BY THE SAME HAND

How Forensic Science Links and Catches Serial Killers

Based on the lecture:
The Methodologies of Serial Killers

MARK ALLEN MYNHIER

BROKEN THREAD PUBLISHING

By the Same Hand: How Forensic Science Links and Catches Serial Killers

This is a work of nonfiction. It draws on the author's professional career, on published case records, and on public data. Accounts of the author's own casework reflect his recollection and are identified as such. Where the author offers a professional interpretation or opinion, it is marked as opinion and not as established fact. Case details drawn from the public record are believed accurate as of the time of writing; readers seeking authoritative detail on any case should consult primary sources.

The views expressed are the author's own and do not represent the views or official position of the Los Angeles Police Department or any other agency with which the author was affiliated.

Published by Broken Thread Publishing LLC

Columbia, SC www.BrokenThreadPublishing.com

ISBN (hardcover): 979-8-9940377-7-5

ISBN (paperback): 979-8-9940377-8-2

First Edition

Printed in the United States of America

For the detectives who keep pulling the file

no one assigned them,

and pay for it out of their own health.

And for one of them in particular,

a friend and a great detective, whom I do not name here

because he valued his privacy,

who chased killers to the far side of the world

and gave the work everything he had.

"Two files land on the same desk. The question is not why. The question is whether they belong to the same hand."

A Note on Method and Sources

This book makes a single argument in many forms: that serial offenders are identified and convicted through evidence and methodology, not through the psychology of why they kill. That distinction governs everything in these pages, including what I was willing to state as fact.

I spent my career as a forensic professional, not as a profiler or a psychologist, and I have tried to stay inside that lane. Where I describe my own casework, I am working from memory, and I say so. Where I draw on the public record, I have worked from primary sources wherever possible: the FBI's Serial Murder Symposium report, the Radford and Florida Gulf Coast University Serial Killer Database, court records, and agency releases. Where a claim is my professional read rather than an established finding, I mark it as opinion.

Statistics in this field move. Databases are revised, victim counts are corrected, and figures that are current at the time of writing will drift. Where a number is likely to change, I have said so rather than pretend to a precision the data cannot support. Readers who want the current figures should consult the sources named in the back matter.

Finally, a word about the victims. They were people, not illustrations of a thesis. I have named them where their names are part of the public record and where naming them honors rather than exploits, and I have declined to name those whose privacy deserves protection, including at least one survivor whose name became public through the worst thing that ever happened to her. The methodology is the subject of this book. The people are the reason it matters.

Acknowledgments

A book that argues the most important work is often done by people whose names never appear in the story would be a poor thing if it did not, at the end, name a few of them.

To Master Sergeant Russell Feeley, my first NCOIC, who taught me before I had any idea I would need to know it what it means to have integrity in your work, and to do a thing correctly whether or not anyone is watching. I lost track of him years ago, and I hope this finds him well.

To Eric Mosher, one of the finest detectives I have ever known, who taught me a great deal about what it takes to be a good forensics man, and who did the work the way it is supposed to be done.

To Pete "Raz" Razanskas whose standing question at the end of a scene, "so, tell me a story," taught me to think through what the evidence was actually saying before I said it out loud. I carried that question into my own career, and asked it at scenes of my own for the rest of it.

To Adam Becknel of the Louisiana State Police, a first-rate forensic technician, a fellow traveler through the standards work of SWGIT and SWGDE, and as fine a guide to New Orleans as a person could ask for.

To my ARC readers, whose early eyes made this a better book than it would otherwise have been.

And to all the unsung forensic technicians I ever worked alongside, the ones who processed the scene, protected the chain, and never appeared in the headline, this book is, among other things, for you. In particular to Larry Holly, who is no longer with us, and to Robert Clark, brother in arms. You did the quiet work. It mattered more than anyone outside the room will ever know.

Contents

Acknowledgments 6

Prologue: The Room Behind the Wall 12

The Women on the Billboards 14

The Number Behind the Number 15

Chapter 1: The Question Every Case Starts With 18

What Linkage Actually Means 19

The Question I Am Not Going to Answer 20

What Evidence Can Tell You, and What It Cannot 22

The Four Things 24

What It Costs to Get This Wrong 25

Chapter 2: Defining the Problem 27

The Definition Nobody Agrees On 27

What It Is Not 29

The Term Itself Is a Little Wrong 30

A Short History 30

The Numbers 31

The Golden Age, and Its End 32

The Vocabulary of Motive 35

Who They Choose 37

Chapter 3: The Myths 39

Myth: They are all evil geniuses. 39

Myth: It is all about sex. 42

Myth: They always hunt near where they live, or work. 43

Myth: They leave signatures. Myth: They collect trophies. 44

Myth: They operate alone. 44

Myth: The majority are men. 45

Myth: Their victims are almost exclusively women. 46

Myth: Once they start, they cannot stop. 46

Myth: They have dozens of victims. 47

What Hollywood Leaves Behind 48

Why the Myths Matter ... 48
Chapter 4: The Four Pillars ... 51
Pillar One: Comfort Zones and Anchor Points ... 51
The anchor point is not always geographic ... 52
The zone is a tendency, not a fence ... 53
Pillar Two: Signature and Modus Operandi ... 53
Signatures only exist in the plural ... 55
The famous signatures are the atypical ones ... 56
The same logic applies beyond homicide ... 56
Pillar Three: Trophies ... 57
Pillar Four: Racial and Cultural Barriers ... 59
What the data actually shows ... 60
The composition of offenders has shifted ... 61
How the Four Work Together ... 61
Chapter 5: Weapons and Method - Capability and Access ... 65
Capability ... 65
Access ... 68
Across Borders ... 69
Reading Method as Evidence ... 74
Chapter 6: The Mobility and Signature Exceptions ... 78
Ted Bundy and the Cost of Mobility ... 78
The early killings were local ... 79
The travel was flight, not hunting ... 80
Florida shows the cost ... 81
What Bundy actually was the exception to ... 82
A note on the bite marks ... 82
BTK and the Manufactured Signature ... 85
Who actually names the killer ... 85
A signature performed for an audience ... 87
Why the manufactured signature is still a signature ... 88
The vanity was the vulnerability ... 89
What the Two Exceptions Teach ... 91

Chapter 7: The Comfort Zone That Isn't a Map 93
The Anchor Point, Where It Was Ordinary 94
Where He Hunted Was Not a Neighborhood 94
The Pillar That Looks Broken and Is Not 96
The Part of the Zone Nobody Maps 97
Victim Selection, Read Honestly 101
The Photographs 102
What This Case Actually Teaches 104
Chapter 8: What the Data Misses, Women Who Kill 106
The Number, and Why It Is Probably Low 106
Money, Not Blood 108
The Structural Parallel 110
The Longer Lineage 112
Aileen Wuornos, and Why She Was the Exception 116
The Reservoir, in Full 116
What This Chapter Actually Argues 117
Chapter 9: Samuel Little and the Undercount Problem 120
The Numbers, and What They Mean 120
Why He Was Invisible 121
The Mobility Inversion 122
How It Finally Broke 123
The Texas Ranger and the Confessions 125
What Little Proves 127
Chapter 10: Zodiac and the Performative Signature 131
What the Record Documents 131
The Confirmed Attacks 133
The Communications 134
What the Communications Were Doing 136
The Cost of Speculation 137
What the Physical Evidence Did 140
The Ongoing Case 141
Chapter 11: The Grim Sleeper and the Room Behind the Wall 145

The Killings, and the Gap That Was Not a Gap 145
Why He Was Called the Grim Sleeper 146
The Break 148
The Surveillance, and the Sample 149
The Room Behind the Wall 150
Ten of Many 151
The Room With the Families 152
Closure 153
Chapter 12: Killer Teams and the Pillars Under Partnership 156
Gerald and Charlene Gallego 158
Doug Clark and Carol Bundy 160
Lawrence Bittaker and Roy Norris 162
Leonard Lake and Charles Ng 165
The Gonzalez Sisters 167
What the Teams Teach 170
Chapter 13: The Venue and the Legend 174
Why a Forensic Book Opens Its History Before the Crime Lab 174
The Man Behind the Legend 176
The Castle That Was Not a Castle 177
The Scheme That Ended Him 178
The Children, and the Letters 179
How Many, Honestly 180
Belle Gunness and the Farm Outside La Porte 181
The Fire, and What the Ground Held 182
The Body That Was Too Small 183
What the Venue Teaches 184
Chapter 14: Synthesis: How We Know 188
What the Pillars Are For 189
The Four Readings, Taken Together 189
What Actually Feeds the Decision 191
The Honest Count 192
Why the Method Exists 193

Epilogue: So What's Next 196

What Is Arriving 197

What Is Leaving 199

Closing the Gap 201

About the Author 203

Prologue: The Room Behind the Wall

We were almost finished.

The arrest had come first, in July of 2010, after twenty-five years and a string of murders that had gone cold, gone quiet, and then started up again. The search warrant came after. By the time we got to the house in South Los Angeles, the work was procedural. Photograph everything. Log everything. Leave with a record so complete that a defense attorney five years later cannot find a gap in it. That was my job on this case. I was the Photographic Supervisor and Lead Photographer, which meant that whatever was found, I was responsible for making sure it was documented exactly as it was found, before anyone touched it.

I was out in the garage. Garages are their own kind of problem for a search team. They accumulate. Shelving, paint cans, tools, boxes of things nobody has opened since the Reagan administration, all of it stacked against walls that nobody has looked at directly in years. You can stand in a two-car garage and not actually see three of the four walls.

One of the officers, and it was an officer rather than a detective, said he thought there might be a door.

I remember what I thought, because I have thought about it many times since. I thought: measure it. Measure the outside of the structure, measure the inside, and if the two numbers do not match, then you know there is space unaccounted for and you can go find it. That is how you would confirm it in about four minutes without pulling the garage apart.

I did not say it out loud. Nobody asked me, and I was not going to walk up to Detective Cliff Shepard, who was running the biggest serial murder investigation in Los Angeles in a generation, and tell him how to conduct his search. He would have laughed, and not unkindly. He would have given me the look that says you have seen too many movies. He would have been right, too. That is exactly where I got it.

They found it the ordinary way, by looking.

It was not a door in any sense that a contractor would recognize. It was a false wall, plywood and clutter arranged to read as the back of the garage, built to push away rather than swing open. There was no knob, no hinge, nothing to see if you were not already suspicious. It was crude, and it had worked for twenty-five years.

Behind it were the photographs.

Nearly a thousand of them, images of women, along with hundreds of hours of home video. Not mounted in albums, not curated the way film and television like to imagine these things, with a killer's scrapbook laid out for a detective to flip through in a single dramatic beat. But not scattered, either. Organized, in the way a person organizes something he intends to keep and intends to return to. That distinction matters, and I will come back to it later in this book, because the difference between what an offender discards and what he keeps is one of the most useful things a scene can tell you.

Elsewhere in the house, not hidden behind anything, we found the gun used in the last murder.

That contrast has stayed with me. The weapon was just in the house. The photographs were behind a wall he had built. Whatever those images were to him, they were the thing worth concealing, and the murder weapon was not.

Nobody had to explain what we were looking at. There was no moment of interpretation, no debate about whether these images were something else, something innocent. Everyone in that garage understood immediately.

What happened next is difficult to describe accurately, and I want to be careful with it, because the easy version is false. Nobody cheered. Nobody high-fived. What went around that garage was quieter than that and, I think, heavier. Satisfied nods. The kind of small, closed-mouth smile that people give each other when something long and grinding has finally turned. Somber, because of what the photographs were and who was in them. But underneath it, every person standing in that garage was cheering on the inside.

We had him.

The Women on the Billboards

That is where a television episode would end, and it is not where the case ended.

We had nearly a thousand photographs and hundreds of hours of video, and we did not know who most of the women in them were.

What followed were two separate public appeals, and they tend to get remembered as one.

The first was about the victims we could name. A digital billboard went up in South Los Angeles carrying their faces in a row across the top, each with a name and a year beneath it, under the words GRIM SLEEPER and, in red letters twice the height of anything else on the board, SUSPECT ARRESTED. Debra Jackson, 1985. Henrietta Wright, 1986. Thomas Steele, 1987. Barbara Ware, 1987. Bernita Sparks, 1987. Mary Lowe, 1987. Lachrica Jefferson, 1988. Alicia Alexander, 1988. Princess Berthomieux, 2002. Valerie McCorvey, 2003. Janecia Peters. At the bottom, a Crime Stoppers hotline, and a credit line for the office of Councilmember Bernard Parks.

There was one more face on that board, shown as a silhouette. She was attacked in 1988 and she survived, the only person who did. Her name is a matter of public record and you could find it in an afternoon if you wanted to. I am not going to put it in this book. Everyone else on that billboard lost the ability to decide what gets attached to their name. She did not, and that decision belongs to her rather than to me.

The second appeal was the harder one, and it did not have names to work with.

The Department released one hundred and eighty of the recovered photographs to the public, a fraction of what was in that compartment. The flyer was headed LAPD NEEDS YOUR HELP, and it described the images as persons photographed by the Grim Sleeper between 1976 and 2010. Below that, a plain sentence stating that these people were not suspects. Then the faces, in a grid, dozens to a page, each one numbered rather than named. Seven. Ten. Sixteen. Nineteen. Twenty-one. The numbers ran into the high eighties and beyond.

That is the detail I have never entirely gotten past. Not a portrait of one woman blown up large enough to read from a moving car, which is what people picture. Dozens of small faces at once, arranged in rows, identified by nothing but a number, because a number was all we had for them.

Very few were ever identified.

The reason is arithmetic, and it is the reason this book exists. Too much time had passed. The oldest of those images dated to the nineteen seventies, more than thirty years before anyone outside that garage saw them. The people who would have recognized those faces had moved, or died, or stopped looking, or never knew the woman was missing in the first place. A photograph taken in 1976 and shown to the public in 2010 is being shown to a different city.

I want to be careful not to turn that into a tidy lesson, because the women in those images were not a lesson. They were people, and most of them are still, as far as the record shows, unnamed. But the honest thing to say about that billboard campaign is that it was an attempt to recover something that had already been lost, and it mostly failed, and it failed because of time.

The Number Behind the Number

Lonnie David Franklin Jr. was convicted of ten murders.

The number of murders the DNA connected him to was officially reported as more than forty. My recollection from the investigation is that the real figure was nearly twice that.

Sit with those numbers for a moment, because the space between them is what this book is about. Ten is what a courtroom proved. Forty-plus, and very probably a good deal more, is what the evidence showed. That gap is not a failure of forensics. Forensics did its job. The gap exists for reasons that are legal, procedural, and strategic, and I will walk through all of them later, including a decision made in that case for reasons most people have never heard, involving a technique that had never been used to arrest and convict anyone in the United States before this case.

But the reason I open with that garage is simpler than any of that.

Every one of those cases had, at some point, been a separate file. A separate scene, a separate date, sometimes a separate decade, sometimes a separate investigating team who never spoke to the team on the other case because they had no reason to think there was another case. A woman in 1985 and a woman in 2002 are two unrelated homicides in a city that has thousands of them, until somebody establishes that they are not.

That is the question this book answers. Not why he did it. There are shelves of books on why, written by people with the training to write them, and I am not one of them. I am not a forensic psychologist and I am going to stay out of that lane, deliberately and completely.

The question I spent a career on is the other one. How do we know? How does a series of murders, separated by years and neighborhoods and investigative jurisdictions, get identified as the work of one person? What does an offender do consistently enough, and unconsciously enough, that it becomes a thread you can pull?

There are answers to that, and they are more concrete than most people expect. They are also almost nothing like what television has taught you to expect. Serial killers get caught, when they get caught, because they behave like people rather than like movie villains. They are creatures of habit. They stay where they are comfortable. They leave things behind, and they take things with them, and both of those are recorded whether they intend it or not.

A man hid a compartment behind a false wall in his own garage for twenty-five years, and kept photographs in it, because he wanted them and could not make himself get rid of them. He left the gun out in the open.

That is not the behavior of a criminal mastermind. That is the behavior of a person who kept souvenirs.

And it is exactly the kind of thing that ends a case.

Chapter 1: The Question Every Case Starts With

Put two homicide files on a desk in front of you.

The first is from 1985. A woman, found in an alley in South Los Angeles. The second is from 2002. A woman, found in South Los Angeles, seventeen years later. Different detectives caught the two cases. Different lab technology processed them, because seventeen years is several generations in forensic science. The detectives on the first case had retired by the time the second one happened. There is no reason on earth for anyone to put those two files side by side, and for seventeen years, nobody did.

Now answer a question. Are you looking at two murders, or are you looking at one murderer?

That question is the entire job. Not the interesting part of the job, not the dramatic part of the job. The job. Everything else in a serial murder investigation is downstream of it, because until you can answer it, you do not have a serial murder investigation at all. You have a stack of unrelated cases in a city that produces hundreds of homicides a year, each one being worked by someone who has no idea the others exist.

So begin where the investigation actually begins, with the two files themselves. What do you have to work with? Not much, and less than you would think. The first file is seventeen years old. The detective who wrote it is retired, possibly dead, and the shorthand in his notes made sense to him and to no one else. The physical evidence was collected under the standards of 1985 and stored under the storage practices of 1985, which is to say some of it has degraded and some of it is simply gone. The second file is fresh, thorough, and built on technology the first detective never had. The two documents do not speak the same language, and nobody has ever asked them to.

That is the ordinary starting condition. The question of whether these are two murders or one murderer is not answered by a flash of insight. It is answered, or not, by whether someone is willing to do the slow work of translating the old file into terms the new one can be compared against, and whether the pieces that would make the comparison survived the seventeen years in between.

The term for answering it is linkage. It is not a glamorous word, and you will not hear it much on television, where the linking tends to happen because a profiler stares at a corkboard until something occurs to him. In practice, linkage is a determination made from evidence, defended in writing, and eventually defended again under cross-examination by a defense attorney whose entire job is to demonstrate that you got it wrong.

What Linkage Actually Means

Linkage is the conclusion that two or more crimes were committed by the same offender. That is all it is. But the standard for reaching that conclusion is higher than most people assume, and the consequences of reaching it incorrectly run in both directions.

Link two cases that are not related, and you have just pointed an investigation at a suspect pool that cannot contain your offender, because you built it out of two different offenders' behavior. You will spend months there. Meanwhile the real one is still working.

Fail to link two cases that are related, and something worse happens. The cases stay separate. Each one gets the resources a single unsolved homicide gets, which in a busy jurisdiction is not much and does not last long. Nobody is looking for a pattern, because officially there is no pattern. The offender continues, and every subsequent victim is, in part, a consequence of that failure.

It is worth being precise about how that second failure actually unfolds, because it does not look like a failure while it is happening. It looks like normal work.

A single unsolved homicide in a busy jurisdiction has a life cycle. It is worked hard for a period measured in weeks, while the scene is fresh and witnesses still remember. Then, absent a break, it slows. The detective who caught it catches three more. The case is not closed and not forgotten, but it moves to the back of a very deep drawer, and the resources it commands drop to almost nothing. This is not negligence. It is triage, and every homicide unit in the country runs on it, because the alternative is to work every case forever and therefore to work none of them well.

Now suppose that case was the first in a series, and the signature in it went unrecognized because there was, as yet, nothing to compare it to. The file goes quiet on schedule. The offender does not. He kills again, in another division, and that case begins its own life cycle, worked by another detective who has no reason to pull a two-year-old file from a drawer across town. Each murder is investigated competently and in isolation. Each one goes quiet on its own schedule. The pattern that would justify pulling them all onto one desk is precisely the thing no single case can reveal, because the pattern only exists in the aggregate, and nobody is looking at the aggregate.

That is the mechanism by which a series runs for a decade. Not one large mistake, but a series of individually reasonable decisions, each of them correct given what the person making it could see. The cost is not paid by the investigation. It is paid by the people the offender reaches in the years before anyone connects the files, and that is the cost this entire discipline exists to reduce.

This is not a hypothetical concern. It is the ordinary condition of these cases. The reason serial murder investigations so often begin years into a series rather than at the start of one is that linkage is genuinely hard, and the evidence that supports it is often not obviously significant at the time it is collected.

Which brings me to the thing I want to establish before anything else in this book.

The Question I Am Not Going to Answer

There is a shelf in every bookstore in America dedicated to why serial killers kill. Some of those books are excellent. A few of them were written by people I have worked alongside or whose work I have relied on professionally. The question of what is happening inside an offender's head is a real question, it has real answers, and those answers have genuine investigative value.

I am not qualified to write that book, and I am not going to pretend otherwise here.

I am not a forensic psychologist. I have never conducted a clinical assessment, I have never testified as an expert on an offender's mental state, and I am not going to speculate about childhood trauma, attachment, or motive structure, because that is somebody else's discipline and they are better at it than I am. Where the psychology becomes unavoidable, and there are a few places in this book where it does, I will tell you whose work I am drawing on and then I will get back to the evidence.

What I did for a living was the other half of it.

I worked for the Los Angeles Police Department from 1998 until 2018, and became a Forensic Supervisor in 2001. Alongside the casework, I spent much of that career on the standards side of the discipline. I sat on the Scientific Working Group on Imaging Technology, and then on the Scientific Working Group on Digital Evidence after the imaging group was wound down in 2015. I chaired the Forensic Photography Committee from 2003 until I retired, and around 2013 and 2014 I worked with the National Institute of Standards and Technology and its Organization of Scientific Area Committees on digital multimedia standards that courts and police departments could adopt if they chose to.

What a Forensic Supervisor does and what the job description says are two different things.

Most of it is resources. My people needed equipment that worked, enough bodies on a shift, training, and someone who would answer a question at two in the morning without making them feel foolish for asking. That is the bulk of the job and none of it is dramatic.

In theory, supervisors handle the harder scenes. In practice, the field photographers were better at the nuts and bolts of field work than the supervisors were, and any supervisor who claims otherwise is describing an organizational chart rather than a crime scene. What we were actually useful for in the field was keeping things running. When a City Councilman or the Chief arrived unannounced, or on a high-profile case arrived exactly as expected, somebody had to talk to them, and it was better for everyone if that somebody was not the photographer trying to work.

The other half was standards. I maintained them for the Division and made sure the work would survive contact with a courtroom. Because I had written them, I was also the one who went to court to testify about them, which suited everybody, since no other supervisor wanted to.

And then there were the cases that needed several photographers working at once. On those, the job was organization: making sure the detectives had what they needed, photographically, at the point they needed it rather than a week later. The Grim Sleeper was one of those.

The standards work is less dry than it sounds, and it is the reason I am the one writing this book rather than a different one. Writing a standard for how digital evidence gets captured, handled, and presented means answering, in advance and in writing, a version of the question this chapter opened with. How do we know what this image shows? How do we know it has not changed since it was taken? How do we know that the thing recovered from a scene in 1985 can still be compared, honestly, to something recovered in 2002? Those are not abstract concerns. They are the difference between evidence that links two cases and evidence a defense attorney takes apart in an afternoon.

The point of listing all that is not to establish that I am impressive. It is to establish what kind of book this is. I spent a career on the evidentiary side of these cases: the scene, the documentation, the physical material, and the chain of reasoning that turns a pile of collected objects into a conclusion a jury will accept. That is the vantage point this book is written from. It is a narrower vantage point than a profiler's, and in some ways a less interesting one. It is also the one that actually closes cases.

What Evidence Can Tell You, and What It Cannot

Television has trained a generation of readers to expect physical evidence to behave like a confession. A hair is recovered, a machine is consulted, a name appears. In practice, evidence rarely produces a name. What it produces is constraint. Each piece of evidence narrows the population of people who could have done this, and the work consists of stacking constraints until the population gets small enough to investigate.

An example makes the logic concrete. Suppose a scene tells you, from the physical evidence alone, that the offender was strong enough to move a body a certain distance without dragging it. That is one constraint. It does not name anyone. It removes a portion of the population and leaves an enormous remainder. Suppose you can also establish, from the same scene, that he had a vehicle, because the body was not found where the person was killed. A second constraint, again naming no one, again removing a portion and leaving a large remainder. Suppose a third thing: that whatever was used is not a weapon most people carry, which tells you something about premeditation and something about access.

None of those three facts identifies a suspect. Any one of them, presented on its own, would strike a jury as nearly worthless. But they do not operate on their own. They operate together, and the population that satisfies all three at once is dramatically smaller than the population that satisfies any one of them. Stack enough of these, and the remainder eventually becomes a group an investigation can actually work through by hand. That is what physical evidence does. It does not hand you the offender. It removes almost everyone who is not the offender, and it keeps removing them, one constraint at a time, until the people who are left are few enough to look at directly.

This is the unglamorous engine underneath every case in this book, and it is worth understanding before we go any further, because the four categories of behavior in the next chapter are simply the most durable constraints of all - the ones an offender cannot stop generating, case after case, because he is not choosing to generate them.

Consider what a crime scene physically is. It is a record of an event, written in a language that includes position, damage, absence, transfer, and time. Some of that record was created deliberately by the offender. Most of it was not. The parts that were not are usually the more useful parts, because a person can control what he intends to do and cannot fully control what he does out of habit.

That distinction, between the intentional and the habitual, is the thread that runs through this entire book. An offender chooses his method. He does not choose, in any meaningful sense, the fact that he is more comfortable in some neighborhoods than others, or that he handles a body a particular way because that is how he has always done it, or that he cannot bring himself to leave a certain kind of object behind. Those are not decisions. Those are patterns, and patterns are what link cases.

A crime scene technician does not walk in looking for a killer. He walks in looking for a record, and he documents that record as completely and as neutrally as he can, on the assumption that some detail he cannot currently interpret will matter to somebody five years from now. That assumption is correct more often than you would think. A great deal of what eventually solves a serial murder case was collected by someone who had no idea, at the time, that they were working a serial murder case.

The Four Things

Strip away the mythology, and four patterns show up in the evidence consistently enough to be useful. They are not a formula, and no offender exhibits all of them cleanly. But they are the four things I look for when I am asked whether two scenes share an author, and they organize the rest of this book.

- Where they hunt. Offenders operate inside a geographic and social comfort zone anchored to a place they know, usually a residence or a workplace. The zone is a constraint, and constraints can be mapped.

- What they leave behind. A signature is a ritual element that is not necessary to complete the crime, and it is one of the few things at a scene that speaks specifically to the offender rather than to the method. It is also routinely confused with modus operandi, which is a different thing entirely and a far weaker basis for linking cases.

- What they take with them. Trophies are the most direct physical connection between an offender and a scene he has otherwise cleaned, and once a suspect is in custody, they are frequently what clears multiple cases at once.

- Who they choose. Victim selection follows patterns of availability, vulnerability, and desirability, and it tends to stay inside racial and cultural lines for reasons that have more to do with where an offender can move without being noticed than with anything else.

Each of those gets a full treatment later. For now, notice what they have in common. Not one of them requires knowing why the offender kills. Every one of them is observable from the outside, recorded in physical evidence, and available to an investigator who never gets within a hundred miles of the inside of a killer's head.

That is not a limitation of the method. That is the method.

What It Costs to Get This Wrong

I want to close this chapter on the stakes, because it is easy to read a book like this as a technical exercise and lose track of what the technique is for.

Go back to the two files on the desk. Seventeen years apart, two women, one city. If somebody links those cases in year two, the investigation that follows is a serial murder investigation, with the resources and urgency and interagency attention that designation brings. If nobody links them until year seventeen, then everything that happened in between happened anyway.

The victims in these cases are not plot devices, and I am going to name them where naming them is appropriate and where it does not intrude on families who did not ask to be in a book. But I want to be clear about the arithmetic, because it is the honest reason methodology matters more than motive. Understanding why an offender kills is intellectually satisfying and occasionally investigatively useful. Establishing that he is the same person who killed someone else, three years ago, in a file nobody has opened since, is what stops him.

The rest of this book is how that gets done.

ON THE RECORD

Established

- **Linkage is the whole job.** Determining that two crimes share one offender is the step every serial investigation depends on; until it is made, there is no serial case, only unconnected files.
- **Getting linkage wrong costs both ways.** A false link points an investigation at a suspect pool that cannot contain the offender. A missed link lets a series continue as separate, under-resourced cases.
- **Evidence constrains; it rarely names.** Physical evidence narrows the population of possible offenders. The work is stacking constraints until that population is small enough to investigate.

The distinction that runs through the book

- **Offenders control what they decide to do, not what they do out of habit.** The intentional parts of a crime are chosen and variable. The habitual parts recur, and the habitual parts are what link cases.

Where this book does not go

- **Not the why.** This is a book about methodology and evidence, not the psychology of motive, which belongs to a different discipline.

Chapter 2: Defining the Problem

Here is a question that sounds simple and is not. How many serial killers are operating in the United States right now?

Before anyone can answer it, they have to agree on what counts. Does a man who kills two people count, or does it take three? Does it matter whether he killed them on the same night? What about a woman who poisoned four husbands over twenty years for the insurance money, never planning a series, never thinking of herself as anything but a person solving a recurring financial problem? What about two people working together?

These are not academic distinctions. Every one of them changes the number, and the number determines whether a task force gets funded.

The Definition Nobody Agrees On

For thirty years, law enforcement, clinicians, and academics used competing definitions of serial murder, differing on victim count, on motive, and on the time between killings. Previous definitions specified anywhere from two to ten victims. That range is not a rounding error. It is the difference between an offender being a statistic in a federal database and being invisible to it.

Congress took one run at fixing this. The Protection of Children from Sexual Predator Act of 1998 (Title 18, United States Code, Chapter 51, Section 1111) defines serial killings as:

> *a series of three or more killings, not less than one of which was committed within the United States, having common characteristics such as to suggest the reasonable possibility that the crimes were committed by the same actor or actors.*

That is a workable definition, and it is not the one investigators use, for a reason worth understanding. The federal definition was never written to describe the crime. It was written to establish the criteria under which the FBI could assist a local agency with an investigation. It is a jurisdictional trigger wearing a definition's clothing. Read it that way and the three-victim threshold makes sense: the Bureau needed a bar high enough to keep federal resources from being spent on every double homicide in America.

In 2005, the FBI convened a Serial Murder Symposium to settle the question properly. The attendees threw out motive as an element, on the grounds that building motive into a definition makes it too complex to apply at the moment you most need it, which is early, when you do not know the motive yet. They lowered the victim threshold, deliberately, because a lower number gives law enforcement more flexibility to commit resources to a case that might be a series. And they produced this:

> *Serial Murder: The unlawful killing of two or more victims by the same offender(s), in separate events.*

Two victims. Separate events. Nothing about motive, nothing about sex, nothing about cooling-off periods or psychological profiles. That is the definition this book uses, and the thing to notice about it is how little it claims. It is not trying to explain the crime. It is trying to tell an investigator, as early as possible, that he may be looking at one offender instead of two unrelated ones. It is a definition built for the moment described in the last chapter, when the second file lands on the desk.

Notice how much of this chapter's opening that plain sentence quietly settles. The woman who poisons four husbands over twenty years is a serial murderer under it, because the deaths are separate events, whatever she believed she was doing at the time. Two people working together are covered by a single parenthetical, offender(s), which carries far more weight than its size suggests, because team killings are common enough that a definition ignoring them would be useless. And whether the murders happened on the same night turns out to be the wrong question; what the definition asks is whether they were separate events, which is not the same thing as separate days. The definition earns its keep not by being profound but by being applicable, one case at a time, at the moment the question actually comes up.

What It Is Not

Two categories get confused with serial murder often enough to be worth clearing away.

Mass murder is generally described as four or more murders occurring during the same incident, in a single location, with no distinctive time period between the deaths. The 1984 San Ysidro McDonald's shooting in San Diego, the 1991 Luby's Restaurant killings in Killeen, Texas, and the 2007 Virginia Tech murders are the examples the Symposium itself used. These are catastrophic crimes. They are not serial murder, and nearly everything in this book is inapplicable to them. A mass murderer does not have a comfort zone in the sense we will discuss, does not develop a signature across scenes, and does not need to be linked to anything, because the linkage question does not arise when all the victims are in one room.

Spree murder is the more interesting exclusion, because the Symposium considered the category and decided to get rid of it. The traditional definition of a spree killer is someone who commits two or more murders without a cooling-off period between them, which is what supposedly distinguishes a spree from a series. The attendees discussed this at length and concluded that the cooling-off period is not a usable concept. It creates arbitrary guidelines. How long is a cooling-off period? A week? A day? Six hours? Nobody could say, and nobody could say it consistently enough for the category to help an investigator do anything. The majority advocated disregarding spree murder as a separate category on the grounds that it provided no real benefit to law enforcement.

I find that decision instructive, and not only for its own sake. It is a good illustration of how the working definitions in this field get made. They are not arrived at by asking what is philosophically true about a killer. They are arrived at by asking what distinction helps somebody standing at a scene at three in the morning. When a category fails that test, it goes.

The Term Itself Is a Little Wrong

While we are being precise, the researchers who maintain the largest database in this field have pointed out that "serial killer" is arguably a misnomer, and that "multiple-event killer" would be more accurate.

The reasoning is sound. The term was originally coined to describe murders that occurred in a series, one leading to the next, a progression. But a substantial number of the offenders in the database committed several murders over a long period of time where the murders were unplanned, unconnected, and not a series in any meaningful sense. A caregiver who kills patients across two decades because each one presented an opportunity is not executing a series. She is repeating a behavior.

I am going to keep using "serial killer," because that is the term everyone uses and inventing new vocabulary would make this book harder to read for no gain. But hold on to the distinction, because it matters later. An offender who is executing a series behaves differently, and leaves different evidence, than an offender who is simply repeating himself. Both get linked the same way. They do not get caught the same way.

A Short History

Jack the Ripper is the first serial killer to catch the world's imagination, and because he was never caught, that fascination never ended. He is also, in a sense, the founding case of this entire field, since the Whitechapel murders of 1888 are among the earliest where investigators explicitly grappled with the linkage problem in public.

He was not the first. Serial killers in America predate him by more than a century. H.H. Holmes is routinely called America's first serial killer, and he was not that either. More than thirty known serial killers operated in America before Holmes, including at least ten women. The Harpe brothers, Micajah and Wiley, ran a killing spree across the western frontier from 1794 to 1799 that the Library of Congress describes as the work of America's first recorded serial killers, decades before Holmes was born. Lydia Sherman, the Derby Poisoner, killed three husbands and a number of children in Connecticut in the 1860s and early 1870s. What Holmes had was not primacy. It was timing and a venue. He built a hotel near the 1893 Chicago World's Fair specifically to kill the people who checked into it, and the combination of a world's fair, a purpose-built murder building, and a national press corps in the same city at the same time made him the first American offender to become a household name.

Notice what that means. The famous cases are not the representative ones. They are the ones with a hook, a nickname, a letter to a newspaper, or a body count large enough to override the ordinary editorial instinct to move on. Every chapter of this book that discusses a well-known case is discussing an outlier, and I will keep saying so, because building a mental model of serial murder out of the famous cases is exactly how people end up believing things that are not true.

The Numbers

Serial killings account for no more than about one percent of all murders in the United States. The FBI's recent Uniform Crime Reporting data puts the country at just over nineteen thousand murders a year, which puts serial murder victims in the range of a couple hundred annually at most.

A couple hundred. In a country of three hundred and forty million people.

I want to be careful here, because there are two wrong conclusions available and people reach for both. The first is that serial murder is therefore not worth the attention it gets. That is wrong for the reason any investigator would give you: a single serial offender generates victims indefinitely until he is stopped, which makes him a fundamentally different resource problem than a single homicide, however tragic. The second wrong conclusion is that the true number must be vastly higher than the recorded one, that there are hundreds of undetected killers operating in the shadows. The honest answer is that the recorded number is certainly an undercount, because these are by definition the cases we know about, but nobody who works with this data seriously believes the undercount is an order of magnitude.

The FBI has long estimated that twenty-five to fifty serial killers are operating in the United States at any given time. That estimate has been repeated so often that it has taken on a life of its own, and it is worth checking against the actual data. The Radford and Florida Gulf Coast University database, which tracks known and identified U.S. serial killers year by year, found an average of thirty-one active per year across 2010 to 2019 using a three-or-more-victim definition, or fifty-three per year using the two-or-more definition.

The FBI's rough estimate, in other words, holds up. That is not always what happens when you check a widely repeated number against a database, and it is worth saying so.

Which, at last, answers the question this chapter opened with. How many serial killers are operating in the United States at any given moment? Somewhere between thirty and fifty, depending on where you set the victim threshold. That is fewer than the mythology wants and more than nothing, and the number worth trusting is not either endpoint but the fact that two independent ways of counting land in roughly the same place.

The Golden Age, and Its End

Between roughly 1970 and 2000, the United States recorded more serial homicides than at any other point in its history. The period sometimes gets called the Golden Age of Serial Killing, which is a distasteful phrase for a real phenomenon.

The scale of it is easier to see in a table than in a sentence. These are known U.S. serial killers, counted by the decade in which their series began. The database's figures begin in 1900, but the phenomenon does not. This is not a modern invention, whatever the Golden Age framing might suggest. Samuel Mason, a river pirate, ran a series from 1797 to 1803, before the table below even opens. Jane Toppan, a nurse, murdered through the 1800s using her profession as cover. Mary Ann Cotton killed more than twenty in England in roughly the same era. The record thins the further back you go, not because the killing was rarer but because the recordkeeping was, and a serial murder that no one connected at the time is a serial murder that never entered any count. What the twentieth century added was not the crime. It was the documentation.

Decade	U.S. serial killers
Pre-1900	documented but uncounted
1900s	53
1910s	62
1920s	70
1930s	67
1940s	61
1950s	93
1960s	255
1970s	673
1980s	840
1990s	729
2000s	438
2010s	215

The line climbs steeply through the sixties, peaks in the 1980s at eight hundred and forty, and then falls off just as steeply. Victim counts follow the same shape, peaking at four hundred and fourteen U.S. serial murder victims in 1987 and generally declining every year since. By the 2010s the decade total was roughly a quarter of what it had been at peak.

Two things are worth saying about that curve.

The first is that the rise and the forensic revolution overlapped almost exactly, and that is not a coincidence in the direction people usually assume. Forensic science did not create serial killers. But the era when serial murder peaked is also the era when DNA typing, systematic evidence protocols, computerized records, and interagency databases were being built, which means the Golden Age is simultaneously the period that produced the most offenders and the period that produced the most complete evidentiary record of them. Nearly everything in this book rests on cases from that window, for that reason.

The second is the decline itself, which is genuinely one of the more interesting findings in the field. The database researchers point to several contributing factors, and none of them is the one people guess.

- Technology closed off entire methods. Insurance-fraud killings, the classic black widow pattern, became far harder to sustain undetected once records were digitized and cross-referenced.
- Parole policy changed. Since 1950, roughly eighteen percent of the U.S. serial killers in the database killed again after being released from prison for a prior homicide, and seventy-nine percent had spent time in jail or prison before their first murder. Longer sentences kept a meaningful number of them off the street.
- The supply of accessible victims contracted. The largest declines in victim types between the 1980s and 1990s and the period after 2000 were hitchhiking-related killings, abductions from shopping centers, and attacks on disabled motorists or people who stopped to help them.

That last one deserves a moment. A generation of Americans stopped hitchhiking, stopped letting their children walk to school alone, and stopped pulling over for a stranger on the shoulder. Much of that cultural change was driven, directly, by publicity about the very killers in this table. The behavior that made those crimes possible became socially extinct, in part because of the crimes themselves.

I will add one observation from the inside, because a data point is worth more when someone who worked the era can tell you what it felt like. My read on the decline is that we are catching more offenders at the first murder than we used to, and the reason is advances in forensics across the board, not any single technique. Better scene documentation, better evidence handling, better records that actually talk to each other between jurisdictions, better everything. What that means in practice is that we have gotten much better at catching the ones who were never very careful to begin with. The unintelligent offender who left evidence everywhere used to get several murders before anyone assembled the picture. Now he often gets one. The intelligent, careful offender is a different story. Him we still do not catch quickly, and sometimes we do not catch him at all. So part of what the declining curve reflects is not that there are fewer killers, but that the ones who end up counted are increasingly the ones who were easy to catch.

An example from my own years on the job shows what the careless end of that spectrum actually looks like. An attractive young woman met the owner of a bar one evening. She flirted with him, and at the end of the night he took her back to his house, where, according to the detectives afterward, the two of them had sex. He fell asleep afterward. She got up, unlocked the front door, and let in her boyfriend and a second man, who robbed and killed him.

It was, in its way, a plan. It was also undone in a single night, because in the hurry to leave she left something behind. This was a few years ago, when people still carried a paper day planner, and hers was on the scene when it was processed. Inside was her driver's license. On another page, in her own handwriting, was the plan itself: the steps for getting into the house, down to a note to borrow a relative's gun.

She was in custody that night. I cannot tell you whether that was her first offense of this kind or whether there would have been others, and my honest read is that it was the first and that there would not have been many, because a person who writes the robbery into the same planner as her driver's license, and then leaves it at the scene, is not someone who builds a long record. Which is the point. Two generations ago, carelessness like that might still have bought several victims before anyone assembled the picture, because the pieces sat in separate files that never met. Now it ends the case the same night.

The Vocabulary of Motive

I said in the last chapter that I am not going to explain why offenders kill. That remains true. But investigators do need a shared vocabulary for motive, because motive determines where a task force looks first and how it allocates people, and a vocabulary is not a theory of the mind.

The Symposium settled on seven broad categories, explicitly non-exclusive, meant as investigative guideposts rather than a full accounting of anyone's interior life:

- Anger, meaning rage or hostility directed at a subgroup or at society generally.
- Criminal enterprise, meaning murder connected to gang, drug, or organized crime activity, committed for status or money.
- Financial gain, meaning direct monetary benefit, from insurance fraud to robbery-homicide.
- Ideology, meaning murder in service of a cause, including racial, ethnic, or gender-based targeting.
- Power or thrill, meaning the offender feels empowered or excited by the act itself.
- Psychosis, meaning killing driven by severe mental illness, including hallucinations or delusions.
- Sexually based, meaning driven by sexual need or desire, whether or not overt sexual contact occurs at the scene.

Note what these categories are for. If a series looks like criminal enterprise, you work informants and known associates. If it looks like financial gain, you work paper: policies, beneficiaries, wills, bank records. If it looks like power or thrill, the paper trail will not help you and the geography probably will. Same crime, entirely different investigation.

This is also the appropriate place to say something about correlation and causation, and then let it go. There is a great deal in this field that is correlated with serial offending and a much smaller amount that anyone can demonstrate causes it. I understand the difference. I am not going to referee that argument, because it is being argued by people with the clinical training to argue it properly, and I am not one of them. Where I cite a pattern, I mean a pattern. If I meant a cause, I would say so, and in this book I almost never will.

Who They Choose

Underneath the seven motive categories, the Symposium's investigators found a consistent logic to victim selection, and this framework is more operationally useful than the motive taxonomy. Three factors:

- Availability. Does the victim's lifestyle, work, or routine bring them within the offender's reach?
- Vulnerability. How exposed is this victim to attack, and how likely is it that an attack would be interrupted or reported?
- Desirability. What about this specific victim appeals to this specific offender, which can involve race, gender, age, physical characteristics, or something considerably more idiosyncratic?

Availability and vulnerability are situational and can be mapped against a city. Desirability is the personal one, and it is the one that produces the patterns that let you link cases. An offender's sense of who is desirable does not usually change much across a series, which is why victim characteristics are among the first things anyone compares when asking whether two cases belong together.

That framework will come back in Chapter 4, where victim selection turns out to be tangled up with geography in a way that is not obvious until you look at the numbers. For now it is enough to notice that all three factors are observable from the outside. You can determine that a victim was available and vulnerable without knowing anything about what was happening inside the offender's head. That is the whole methodological bet of this book, and the next chapter is about everything people believe instead.

ON THE RECORD

Established

- **There is a working definition and a legal one, and they differ.** The FBI's two-victim, separate-events definition is the operational one. The federal three-victim standard was written as a jurisdictional trigger for FBI assistance, not as a description of the crime.

- **Serial murder is rare.** It accounts for no more than about one percent of U.S. murders, and an estimated twenty-five to fifty offenders are active at any time, a figure the database roughly confirms.
- **This is not a modern phenomenon.** Serial killers predate the country. Documented cases run back well before 1900; the record thins going back not because the crime was rarer but because the recordkeeping was.
- **The Golden Age rose and fell.** Recorded serial homicide peaked in the 1980s and has fallen sharply since, for reasons including better forensics, longer sentences, and the disappearance of high-risk victim behavior like hitchhiking.

Myth

- **That H.H.** Holmes was America's first. More than thirty known offenders, including at least ten women, preceded him. He was the first to become famous, not the first to exist.
- **That mass murder and serial murder are the same problem.** They are not, and almost nothing in this book applies to a single-location, single-event mass killing.

Still unsettled

- **The exact current murder baseline.** The annual U.S. total moves year to year and has been dropping fast; any single figure is a snapshot, not a constant.

Chapter 3: The Myths

Almost everything the average person believes about serial killers came from a screen.

That is not a criticism of the audience. It is a structural problem. The real information lives in federal monographs, university databases, and case files, none of which are written to be read for pleasure. The entertaining version is free, ubiquitous, and extremely well made. Of course it won.

The trouble is that the entertaining version is not merely inaccurate. It is inaccurate in a specific direction. Fiction needs an antagonist worth the protagonist's time, so the fictional serial killer is brilliant, theatrical, mobile, and unpredictable. The real ones are, with rare exceptions, none of those things. Every myth in this chapter makes the offender more interesting than he is, and every one of them, taken seriously by an investigator, points an investigation somewhere useless.

So let us go through them.

Myth: They are all evil geniuses.

This one is nearly the opposite of the truth, and we can be specific about it, because intelligence tracks with method in a way that is measurable.

The Radford and Florida Gulf Coast University database has recorded IQ scores for 271 serial killers. The average is 94.5, the median 86. For context, the population average is 100 by construction. Serial killers are, as a group, below average by a few points on the mean and further below on the median, which is to say indistinguishable from the general public in any way that would matter if you met one, and, if anything, slightly duller than the room.

The interesting part is the spread by method. The table below gives the average IQ for each recorded method, along with N, meaning the number of offenders each average is based on. That number matters here, because some of the rows rest on very few people:

Method	Average IQ	N

Bomb	140.3	3
Strangle / Bludgeon	108.8	8
Strangle / Shoot	105.8	6
Poison	100.0	1
Strangle	96.7	41
Stab / Shoot	95.0	26
Stab	92.3	25
Shoot	90.7	61
Strangle / Stab	90.2	14
Bludgeon / Shoot	87.1	11
Bludgeon / Stab	85.5	11
Bludgeon	79.1	10

Read down the column and one relationship stands out. The methods that put distance between the offender and the victim cluster at the top. The methods that require the offender to be within arm's reach cluster at the bottom. Bombs, poison, and the compound remote methods sit above the mean; single-implement, close-contact methods sit below. Intelligence, in these numbers, is tracking how far from the victim the offender is willing or able to be.

Bombers score highest by a wide margin, and the reason is not mysterious: building a functioning explosive device that works when it is supposed to, and does not detonate in your own hands first, requires technical competence that most people simply do not have. Ted Kaczynski, the Unabomber, held a doctorate in mathematics from the University of Michigan and had held an assistant professorship at Berkeley before he moved to a cabin in Montana.

Kaczynski is worth pausing on, because he is a useful edge case rather than a clean example. Over seventeen years he built and delivered sixteen bombs, and they killed three people. He is famous, and he is frequently cited in exactly this context, but by the raw arithmetic of victims he barely satisfies the definition of a serial killer at all. What made him extraordinarily hard to catch was not a high body count. It was his method. He killed remotely. He mailed or planted his devices and was nowhere near them when they went off, which means he left almost none of the evidence that the rest of this book is about. No comfort zone in the usual sense, no scene he was present at, no victim who ever saw him. The bomb category scores highest on intelligence precisely because remote, technical killing selects for the small number of offenders who can manage it, and that same remoteness is what makes those offenders the exception to nearly every method in these pages.

At the other end, offenders who bludgeon average 79.1, which is meaningfully below the group mean and more than fifteen points below the population average. That also fits. Bludgeoning requires no planning, no acquisition, no skill, and no tool that is not already in the room.

One caution about that table, and it applies to a great deal of the data in this book. Those averages are drawn from very different sample sizes, which is why the N column is printed alongside them. The bomb figure rests on three people. The poison figure rests on one. The shoot and strangle figures rest on dozens. A mean built from three cases would move fifteen or twenty points if two more offenders were added; a mean built from sixty is stable. I flag this because the top-line numbers are often quoted without it, and a mean built from a handful of cases is a weaker claim than a mean built from tens. The direction of the finding is solid. The precision implied by a figure like 140.3 is not.

There is more to say about method as evidence, and this chapter is not the place to say it. What the IQ table hints at is that method choice reveals something about an offender that goes past intelligence in the ordinary sense - it reveals what he is capable of and, just as importantly, what is available to him. That argument gets its full treatment in Chapter 5, alongside the question of why the same period and the same country produce very different weapon choices in different offenders. For now, the point that belongs in a chapter about myths is smaller: the evil-genius picture is wrong on the numbers, and where intelligence does track upward it tracks with a specific kind of distance from the crime rather than with cleverness in general.

What the data does not support, at all, is the criminal mastermind. If you built a mental image of serial killers from the Radford numbers, you would picture someone entirely ordinary, and you would be right far more often than the person picturing Hannibal Lecter.

Myth: It is all about sex.

The popular version of this myth has two parts: that the motive is always sexual, and that the victims are predominantly sex workers. Both are wrong, and the database is unusually clear on the second one.

The largest single category of U.S. serial killer victims is home or home invasion, at 15.7 percent. Family members account for 10.8 percent. Employees or customers, 9.3 percent. Friends or acquaintances, 8.9 percent. Victims categorized as prostitutes account for 8.5 percent.

Read that again. Fewer than one in ten. A serial killer in the United States is nearly twice as likely to kill a family member as a sex worker.

The myth persists because of visibility rather than frequency. Cases involving sex workers are overrepresented in the cases that become famous, partly because those series tend to run longer before detection, for reasons Chapter 9 will get into, and a series that runs longer produces more victims, more press, and more cultural residue.

There is a second reason, and it has nothing to do with the data and everything to do with why these stories get told. A sexually motivated murder is more salacious than a killing for insurance money, and salacious sells. But it also does something more respectable-looking than titillation: it carries a warning. The story of the woman who went home with a stranger and did not come back is a morality tale as much as a crime report, and it gets repeated partly because it seems to instruct. Both impulses, the prurient and the protective, push in the same direction, toward a picture of serial murder as fundamentally about sex. The data does not support the picture. The picture endures anyway, because it entertains and it warns at the same time, and that is a durable combination.

As for motive, when incarcerated serial offenders are interviewed, more than sixty percent report that they were motivated by enjoyment, financial gain, or some combination of the two. The answer they give is often a variation of wanting to do it because it seemed like fun, which is unsatisfying as an explanation and appears to be sincere. Sexual motivation is real and it is common. It is not the default.

Myth: They always hunt near where they live, or work.

This one is mostly true, and I use the word hunt intentionally. It also has an exception large enough to be worth understanding, which is why the heading includes the words "or work."

Most serial killers have very defined geographic areas of operation, conducting their killings inside comfort zones defined by an anchor point, which the FBI describes as a place of residence, employment, or the residence of a relative. Very few travel interstate to kill. The ones who do fall into a small number of categories: itinerant individuals who move from place to place, homeless individuals living transiently, and people whose employment involves interstate or transnational travel, such as truck drivers or military personnel.

That third category is the one that complicates the myth, and it is why the comfort zone should never be understood as purely residential. For a long-haul trucker, the comfort zone is the road. He is not a stranger anywhere on his route. The truck stops, the rest areas, and the on-ramps are as familiar to him as a neighborhood is to anyone else, and he has a professional reason to be at any of them at three in the morning.

Two cases in the database illustrate the pattern. Robert Ben Rhoades, known as the Truck Stop Killer, was active from 1975 to 1990, with three murders proven and considerably more suspected. 'ngel Maturino Res'ndiz, called the Railroad Killer, was active from 1986 to 1999, with ten proven and more suspected, and used his access to a truck as part of the crimes themselves.

The FBI also notes something worth holding on to: offenders will at times spiral their activity outward, beyond the established comfort zone, either as confidence grows through experience or specifically to avoid detection. A comfort zone is a tendency, not a fence. An investigator who treats the zone as a hard boundary will miss the case that stepped outside it, and the ones that step outside it are frequently the later ones, after the offender has had practice.

Myth: They leave signatures. Myth: They collect trophies.

Both true. Both are load-bearing enough that they get a full treatment in Chapter 4, along with the distinction between a signature and a modus operandi, which is the single most consequential piece of terminology in this book and the one most often gotten wrong.

Myth: They operate alone.

Mostly, but not always, and the exception is more common than most people assume.

The Radford database defines what these arrangements look like. Team killers typically involve between two and four people, linked by being family, lovers, or, in the database's framing, accomplices, a word worth preferring over friends, because the bond is not always friendship. Some of these offenders recruit their partners, drawing in an admirer or a follower rather than a peer, which produces a very different dynamic than two equals killing together. That is a different category from organizational killing, where the murders are sanctioned by a gang, criminal enterprise, or cult, which the researchers treat as fundamentally different from individual and team killing and are moving toward separating out of the dataset entirely.

The best-known team case is Karla Homolka and her husband Paul Bernardo, who raped and murdered at least three minors in Ontario between 1990 and 1992, including Homolka's own sister.

Investigatively, partnered offenders matter for a reason that has nothing to do with psychology. Two people leave more evidence than one. They also introduce a failure point that a solo offender does not have, because the case can break through one of them rather than through the physical evidence. But an investigator who has assumed a lone offender from the start will read a scene wrong: two sets of behaviors at one location can look like inconsistency in a single offender rather than what it is.

Myth: The majority are men.

True, and the real figure is both smaller than most people assume and moving.

Women account for roughly nine to eleven percent of known serial killers. More interesting than the number is the trend. Before 1930, close to a third of known serial killers were women. Since 1980, the figure has fallen to around six percent, and it has been declining for a century.

The persistent belief that female serial killers are a modern curiosity, or barely exist at all, owes something specific to Hollywood. The 2003 film Monster dramatized the case of Aileen Wuornos, and the marketing around it leaned on the idea that she was America's first female serial killer. She was not. She was not close. Female serial killers predate the United States itself. What Wuornos was, arguably, is the first female serial killer to fit the male template, killing strangers with a firearm rather than poisoning intimates for money, which is part of why she read as unprecedented when she was nothing of the kind. The women who came before her are less famous precisely because their methods were quieter, and quieter is exactly what the record has always had trouble seeing.

I want to be careful about what the shrinking percentage does and does not mean, because it is easy to misread. This is a change in the composition of a shrinking population, not evidence that women have become less capable of the crime. The methods historically associated with female offenders, poisoning in particular and killings motivated by financial gain, are precisely the methods that modern record-keeping, toxicology, and insurance investigation have made hardest to sustain undetected. Chapter 2 covered that decline. The gender shift appears to be one of its effects.

I worked one of these cases, and it taught me more about how female offenders operate, and how easily they are underestimated, than any statistic could. The motive was the classic one for a female serial killer: money. She would seduce older, wealthier men, and then, once she was inside their lives, a couple of her associates would come into the house, bind the victim, and force him to give up his PIN numbers so the accounts could be emptied. Then they would tape him up, drive him out, and drop him into a Los Angeles reservoir.

What broke the case was a single shoe print. A Sheriff's Deputy had photographed it at one location, without a ruler in the frame and without a scale, which meant the photograph on its own was close to useless for establishing a measurement. So I went back to the spot and measured the knowns, the fixed objects in the scene whose dimensions I could establish, poles and the like, and used them to work back to the unknown: her shoe size, and from there a potential brand. That reconstruction was solid enough to support a search warrant, and the search warrant is how she was caught.

I will not pretend that case is representative. It is not; it is unusually organized, and most female offenders do not run a crew. But it sits directly on top of the myth this section is about. She was not suspected early, in part because the picture in everyone's head of a serial killer did not include a woman seducing men for their bank balances and outsourcing the violence. When women do kill serially, financial gain is far more often the driving motive than it is for men, and the willingness to overlook a woman as a suspect is, itself, part of the method's success.

Myth: Their victims are almost exclusively women.

No. The split is close to even, with approximately 49 percent of serial killer victims male and 51 percent female, per the Psychology Today summary of the database.

Some offenders target one gender exclusively. Others show no discernible pattern at all. Richard Ramirez, the Night Stalker, killed men and women, the young and the elderly, across multiple races and ethnicities. His victim list is close to random, which is itself a finding: an offender with no consistent victim preference is much harder to link, because victim characteristics are one of the first things anyone compares when asking whether two cases belong together.

Myth: Once they start, they cannot stop.

This one is not in most popular accounts, and it should be, because it is operationally the most dangerous myth in the chapter.

Some serial killers stop killing entirely, on their own, before anyone catches them. The FBI documents circumstances that appear to inhibit further offending: increased involvement in family activities, sexual substitution, and other diversions.

Dennis Rader, BTK, murdered ten victims between 1974 and 1991. He killed no one after 1991 and was not captured until 2005, a gap of fourteen years. In interviews after his arrest he described substituting auto-erotic activity for the killings. Jeffrey Gorton killed his first victim in 1986 and his second in 1991, killed no one afterward, and was captured in 2002.

The common thread in these cases, and it is worth stating as a possibility rather than a certainty, is that the offender did not lose the underlying drive so much as redirect it. The FBI's own framing points that way: the diversions it lists, family involvement, sexual substitution, and the rest, are replacements, not cures. It is reasonable to suspect that a man who stops killing has, in many cases, found another fixation that occupies the same place, whether that is a compulsion, a relationship, or something else that absorbs him. That does not make him safe. It makes him quiet, which is a different thing, and quiet is exactly the condition that lets a case go cold.

Consider what that means for an unsolved series. When the murders stop, the natural inference inside a squad room is that the offender died, moved away, or went to prison for something else. Those are all reasonable inferences. They are also the inferences that let a case go cold while the offender is still living twelve miles away. The killings stopping is not evidence that the offender stopped existing.

Myth: They have dozens of victims.

Some do. Most do not. Most serial killers kill fewer than eight people, and the number of victims per offender has fallen sharply over the past seventy years. In 1950, thirty-eight percent of serial killers had five or more victims. That figure is now around thirteen percent.

The explanation is not that offenders have become less ambitious. It is that they get caught sooner. Better investigative technique, DNA, video surveillance, and communication between jurisdictions all shorten the interval between the first murder and the arrest, and every case in this book that produced an enormous body count did so partly because it ran for years without anyone establishing that the cases belonged together.

Which is the point of the whole book, arriving from a different direction. Body count is not a measure of an offender's capability. It is a measure of how long the linkage took.

What Hollywood Leaves Behind

A brief word on the theatrical details, because they are worth quantifying rather than merely dismissing.

Among U.S. serial killers in the database, cannibalism appears in around two percent of cases involving white offenders and well under one percent of cases involving black offenders. Necrophilia appears in roughly three percent and one percent respectively. Drinking a victim's blood appears in under one percent in both groups.

These behaviors are real. They are also vanishingly rare, and they are massively overrepresented in fiction precisely because they are rare, which is what makes them dramatic. Dahmer is famous partly because Dahmer is unusual. Building a general model of serial murder out of the most extreme cases is like forming a picture of commercial aviation from crash footage.

Why the Myths Matter

None of this is trivia. Every myth in this chapter, believed by someone with a caseload, sends an investigation the wrong direction.

It is worth naming what these myths have in common, because the pattern is consistent. Almost none of them is a pure fabrication. Each one is a misrepresentation or an exaggeration of something with a grain of truth in it. Some serial killers are intelligent, so the myth inflates that into evil genius. Some are sexually motivated, so the myth expands that into all of them. Some travel, some collect trophies, some are women, and in each case a real but limited fact has been stretched until it covers cases it does not fit. The stretching is not random. It happens in the direction that makes a better story, whether the goal is a dramatic television episode or a cautionary tale that seems to teach a lesson. Reality is more particular and less tidy than either purpose wants it to be, and the distortion is the cost of making it fit.

Assume an evil genius, and you overlook the ordinary suspect who is standing in plain view, because he does not seem clever enough. Assume the motive is sexual, and you deprioritize the financial paper trail that would have closed the case in a week. Assume a lone offender, and you stop looking after you have one person in custody. Assume the killer must be a man, and roughly one case in ten becomes invisible to you. Assume the murders stopped because the offender is gone, and you close the file on someone who is still in the neighborhood.

And assume that a serial killer looks like a serial killer, and you will walk past him, because he looks like everybody else. That is the finding underneath every number in this chapter, and it is the reason the next four chapters are about behavior rather than about people. You cannot identify these offenders by what they are. You can identify them by what they repeatedly do.

ON THE RECORD

Established

- **Intelligence tracks with method, not mastermind status.** The average serial-killer IQ is a few points below the population mean, and the median lower still. It varies by method, with technical, remote methods scoring higher and crude, close-contact ones lower.
- **Victims are not predominantly sex workers.** A U.S. serial killer is nearly twice as likely to kill a family member as a sex worker; the largest victim category is home or home invasion.
- **Most hunt near where they live or work.** The comfort zone is real. The main exceptions are offenders whose work is the road, such as long-haul truckers.
- **Some stop on their own.** A number of offenders cease killing before capture, apparently by redirecting the drive into another fixation. Stopping is not proof the offender is gone.

- **Most have fewer victims than the legend suggests.** Most kill fewer than eight, and the share with five or more has fallen sharply as offenders get caught sooner.

Myth

- **The evil genius.** Real, but rare enough to be the exception rather than the rule.
- **That it is always about sex.** Motive is varied: money, thrill, anger, and more. The sex-motive myth endures because it is both salacious and moralizing.
- **That they always operate alone.** A meaningful share kill in teams of two to four, linked as family, lovers, or accomplices, sometimes a recruited follower rather than a peer.
- **That they are all men.** Roughly nine to eleven percent are women, and that share has been falling for a century. The film Monster's claim that Aileen Wuornos was America's first female serial killer is false; female serial killers predate the nation.
- **That victims are almost all women.** The split is close to even, roughly forty-nine percent male and fifty-one percent female.

The pattern underneath the myths

- **Each myth is a grain of truth, stretched.** Not fabrications but exaggerations, pulled in whatever direction makes a better story or a tidier moral lesson.

Chapter 4: The Four Pillars

An offender controls what he decides to do. He does not control what he does without deciding.

That sentence is the whole chapter. Everything that follows is four specific applications of it, four categories of behavior that persist across an offender's crimes because they are not, in any useful sense, chosen. Where he is comfortable. What he needs to do that the crime does not require. What he cannot leave behind. Who he is able to approach without being noticed.

These are the four things I look at when somebody asks whether two scenes share an author. None of them requires knowing anything about the inside of the offender's head. All of them are observable from the outside, and all of them are recorded, one way or another, in physical evidence.

Pillar One: Comfort Zones and Anchor Points

Most serial killers operate inside a well-defined geographic area. The FBI describes this as a comfort zone, and it is usually organized around an anchor point: a place of residence, a place of employment, or the residence of a relative.

The logic is not complicated. A person moves confidently in a place he knows. He knows which streets are watched and which are not, where the lighting fails, when the foot traffic thins, and which route out does not pass a busy intersection. He also has a reason to be there, which matters more than any of the rest of it. A man walking through his own neighborhood at two in the morning is a man walking home. The same man in a neighborhood twenty miles away is a stranger, and strangers get noticed and remembered.

Jack the Ripper is the textbook case. The Whitechapel murders of 1888 were confined to a small district of London, and that concentration is precisely what made them recognizable as a series in the first place. Bundy is the counterexample everyone reaches for, killing across Washington, Utah, Florida, Colorado, Oregon, Idaho, and California, though much of that range came while he was on the run after two escapes from custody, a distinction Chapter 6 returns to. Interstate mobility on that scale is rare, and it is rarer still that it reflects a genuine absence of a comfort zone rather than a fugitive's forced movement.

Two refinements matter more than the basic idea, because the basic idea is where most accounts stop.

The anchor point is not always geographic

For Jeffrey Dahmer, the anchor was not an address. It was a set of bars. His comfort zone was social rather than spatial, and it functioned exactly the way a neighborhood would: he knew the norms, he was not conspicuous, and he had an unremarkable reason to be present.

This generalizes further than people expect. An anchor can be a workplace, a hospital ward, a boarding house, a church, a trucking route, a shift. Any bounded environment where an offender is a familiar presence rather than an anomaly will do the same work. When a series of deaths clusters inside a nursing facility, the anchor point is the facility, and the investigation looks nothing like a geographic profile even though the underlying principle is identical.

The clearest illustrations come from healthcare. When the anchor point is a hospital ward or a nursing home, the offender's presence is not merely unremarked but professionally required, and the population of possible victims is walked past every shift. Charles Cullen, a nurse convicted in 2006, admitted to killing patients across at least nine hospitals and nursing homes in Pennsylvania and New Jersey over sixteen years. His comfort zone was not a neighborhood. It was a role. A man in scrubs at three in the morning does not need an excuse to be on the floor, and does not need an alibi for being near the deceased, because the deceased were in his professional care. What broke that pattern was not surveillance of a geographic area. It was cross-institutional records - pharmacy audits at multiple facilities that finally added up when someone looked at them together. That is the same linkage problem from Chapter 1, in a different setting. The comfort zone stayed intact for sixteen years precisely because no single hospital could see the whole of it.

A workplace anchor requires a different investigative posture than a geographic one, because the boundary of the zone is drawn by employment records, credentialing, and shift schedules rather than by neighborhoods. What that means practically is that a case with no geographic pattern is not a case with no anchor. It is a case where the anchor is somewhere else, and the question worth asking is what environment this offender moved through unremarked.

What this means practically is that when you cannot find a geographic pattern, you have not established that there is no comfort zone. You have established that the comfort zone is not a place.

The zone is a tendency, not a fence

The FBI notes that offenders will at times spiral their activity outward, beyond the established zone, either as confidence grows through experience or specifically to avoid detection.

That second reason deserves attention, because it is the one that breaks investigations. An offender who has watched police activity concentrate in his neighborhood has an obvious incentive to work somewhere else for a while. If your working assumption is that the offender lives inside the cluster, the cases that fall outside it look like a different person, and you have just unlinked two cases that belong together.

So the comfort zone is a strong prior and a weak boundary. It tells you where to start. It does not tell you where to stop.

Pillar Two: Signature and Modus Operandi

This is the most consequential distinction in the book, and the one that gets confused most often, including by people who ought to know better.

Modus operandi is method. It is how the offender accomplishes the crime: how he approaches, how he controls, how he leaves. John Douglas, the FBI behavioral analyst whose work most of the popular vocabulary comes from, describes M.O. as learned and dynamic. An offender who runs into a problem during one crime adjusts his method for the next one. He gets better at it. That is what learned behavior does.

Which produces the rule that follows from it, and it is a rule I have watched people break: you should not link cases on modus operandi alone. Method changes over time within a single offender, and method is also shared by offenders who have nothing to do with each other. Two burglars who both enter through sliding glass doors have not thereby become the same burglar. They have both discovered that sliding glass doors are easy.

A signature is something else entirely. Douglas defines it as a ritual, and he says he coined the term for this purpose. In his words, the signature is **the ritual that is unique to the offender**, and it is the thing worth looking for. The defining feature is that it is not necessary. It does not advance the crime. Frequently it makes the crime harder or riskier, and the offender does it anyway.

Douglas illustrates the distinction with two robberies, and it is the clearest example I know of, partly because neither case is a homicide.

In both robberies, the offender made his captives undress. Identical behavior, described identically in a report. But in the first case, the purpose was practical: people who have been stripped are embarrassed and preoccupied, they do not look closely at the man robbing them, and they make poor eyewitnesses afterward. That is method. It serves the crime.

In the second case, the offender posed the victims and photographed them. Nothing about that advanced the robbery. It kept him inside the building longer, which increased his chance of being caught, and he did it regardless. That is signature. It served him.

Same observable act, undressing the victims, on opposite sides of the line. Which is why reading a scene is not a matter of cataloguing behaviors. It is a matter of asking, behavior by behavior, whether this served the crime or served the offender.

The stakes of the distinction are not academic. Consider what happens when an investigator gets it wrong in either direction. Link two cases on shared M.O. - two women found with the same type of ligature, in similar postures, by roadsides in the same region - and you may have joined two entirely unrelated offenders who both happen to work in the way that most sexual homicides go, because that combination of behaviors is not rare. The linkage looks strong, the false suspect pool feels real, and the actual offender in each case continues without ever coming near your investigation. Fail to link two cases on shared signature, on the other hand, because the M.O. differs - one offender changed weapons between his second and third murder, and the surface details of the two scenes now look nothing alike - and you have missed a series that was in front of you, because the ritual you should have been reading was buried in details that were not obviously connected to method at all. The rule is not that M.O. never matters; it does, and it belongs in the record. The rule is that M.O. alone is not enough weight to hang a linkage on, and that a signature is worth more than any three matched M.O. elements combined, because the signature is a thing the offender needed and the M.O. is a thing the crime needed.

Signatures only exist in the plural

There is a constraint on all of this that gets lost in dramatizations, and it is the reason this pillar depends on the linkage problem rather than solving it.

You cannot identify a signature from one case. Douglas is explicit about this: the ritual is only visible once it starts recurring. A posed body at a single scene is an unexplained detail. The same posing at a second scene is a signature. Until the second case exists and someone puts the two files side by side, there is nothing to see.

This is worth sitting with, because it means the tool that links cases requires linked cases to become visible. In practice, the first case in any series is nearly always worked as an isolated homicide, and the signature in it is invisible, sitting in a report, correctly documented and entirely unremarkable, waiting for a second case to give it meaning. That is not a failure of anyone's competence. It is the structure of the problem.

It is also the strongest argument I know for documenting everything at a scene, including the details that appear to mean nothing. The technician who photographs an oddly arranged object in 1985 is not being thorough for its own sake. He is leaving something for the person who opens the file in 2002.

The famous signatures are the atypical ones

Jack the Ripper and the Zodiac Killer sent letters. The Unabomber had a manifesto. Dennis Rader, BTK, built a signature deliberately, wanted his crimes recognized as his, was frustrated when they were not, and took active steps to make sure the connection was made.

Notice what all of those have in common. They are communications. They were meant to be seen, and they were meant to be attributed. That is not what most signatures are. Most signatures are private, and the offender would prefer you did not notice them at all. The term itself is unfortunate for this reason, since it suggests an artist adding a flourish to finished work. A signature is closer to an involuntary imprint, and it shows up most clearly on the crimes that went wrong, where the offender was rushed or interrupted and the practiced parts of his method fell away, leaving only the parts he could not skip.

The same logic applies beyond homicide

Both of the robbery cases above involve offenders who did not kill anyone. That is not incidental to the example; it is the point of including it. Signature behavior is not a property of murder. It is a property of repeat offenders, and it appears anywhere a person commits the same category of crime more than once and cannot stop doing the unnecessary part.

This has direct consequences for serial sexual assault. The same analysis applies without modification: separate a rapist's method from his ritual, link on the ritual, disregard the method, and understand that neither will be visible until there is a second case. And because sexual assault is far more frequently survived than homicide, these cases carry something homicide cases do not, which is a witness who can describe behavior that never made it into physical evidence.

I want to be careful not to overstate the connection. I am not claiming that serial killers begin as serial rapists, or that the two populations are the same people at different stages. What I am saying is narrower and better supported: the two crimes share the underlying structure that makes linkage possible. A repeat offender leaves a ritual, the ritual is separable from the method, and the ritual is what ties the cases together. That is as true of a series of sexual assaults as it is of a series of murders, and an investigator who understands it in one context already understands it in the other.

Pillar Three: Trophies

Lonnie Franklin, Jr. photographed his victims. Those photographs helped convict him, and they are also the reason anyone knows he had more victims than he was tried for.

A trophy is an object an offender removes from a scene and keeps. It is not proceeds, and the distinction matters, because the two look identical in an evidence log and behave completely differently in an investigation. Proceeds get sold, spent, or discarded. Trophies get kept, which is precisely what makes them useful.

A study conducted for the FBI examined 480 cases of serial murder and recorded what was taken from the scene:

Item taken	Percentage of cases
Clothing or shoes	48.5
Jewelry	31.7
Wallet or purse	23.6
Money	20.5

Personal items outrank money, and it is not close. Clothing appears in nearly half of cases; cash in a fifth. And contrary to almost every fictional treatment of this subject, collecting body parts is not common.

There are no reliable figures on what share of serial killers take trophies. The honest answer is that most do, in some form. What I can tell you with confidence is the investigative consequence, which is the reason this pillar earns its place.

An offender who keeps things accumulates a physical archive of his own crimes, in his possession, under his control, for as long as he remains free. Every trophy is an item that connects a specific person to a specific victim, and unlike biological evidence, a trophy does not require the offender to have made a mistake. He acquired it deliberately, and he kept it deliberately, and the longer he operates the more of them there are.

Which is why the search warrant is frequently the moment a case stops being about one murder. A single execution of a warrant can clear cases across decades, in multiple jurisdictions, that no one had connected. The garage in the prologue is exactly this. A concealed compartment in a private residence held the connective tissue for a series that had been worked as unrelated homicides for twenty-five years.

The Prologue of this book is that moment. What was behind the false wall in that garage in South Los Angeles was not a single trophy tied to a single victim; it was hundreds of photographs and hours of video, kept for twenty-five years, organized rather than discarded, concealed rather than displayed. The gun that had been used in the most recent murder was somewhere else entirely, out in the open. That contrast is not a curiosity. It is the pattern this pillar describes, made physical. What an offender is willing to keep on a shelf, and what an offender is willing to hide behind plywood, are two different categories of object, and the distance between them tells you what he values. In that case, and in others of its kind, the concealed archive was worth more to him than the weapon that produced it. That is what a trophy is, in the operational sense. It is also, as the case chapters will show, the reason a single warrant can end a series.

Why offenders keep these things is outside my lane and I am going to leave it there. The commonly offered explanations are reliving the event, a form of private bragging, and maintaining a connection to the victim. Those may all be true and I have no professional basis to adjudicate among them. What is not in dispute is the operational fact: the object exists, the offender keeps it, and keeping it is how he is eventually tied to everything he did.

This is also where the search warrant does quiet, underappreciated work. A warrant is often written broadly, authorizing seizure of evidence related to the offense and any ancillary evidence connected to the case, and that breadth is deliberate. When we go in, we usually do not know what the trophy is. We know only that there is likely to be one, because most offenders keep something. So the warrant has to leave room to recognize and seize an object whose significance is not obvious on its face, a box of photographs, a piece of jewelry that matches no one in the house, a garment that does not belong. I have seen the trophy turn out to be almost anything. What stays constant is that the offender almost always has one, and that the document authorizing the search has to be written to catch a thing we cannot describe in advance.

Pillar Four: Racial and Cultural Barriers

Offenders tend to kill within their own racial and cultural groups. This pattern is real, it is well documented, and it is the pillar most likely to be misunderstood, so I want to be precise about both what it says and what it does not.

Start with why it exists, because the mechanism explains the exceptions. This is not a claim about prejudice or about who an offender considers acceptable to kill. It is the comfort zone again, viewed from a different angle. An offender operates where he is unremarkable, and in most American cities, race and culture shape where a given person is unremarkable at least as strongly as geography does. A man who does not belong in a neighborhood is noticed, remembered, and described. That is the entire mechanism.

Which is also why the barrier is not strictly racial. Consider a Hispanic child raised from early childhood in a Caucasian household, who may identify far more with the culture he was raised in than with his ethnic background. What defines the comfort zone is fluency, not ancestry. The same applies to subculture. Dahmer's victims came overwhelmingly from the bars he frequented himself, and moving through that environment without drawing attention requires knowing its norms, which is learned rather than inherited.

It is worth being precise about which comfort zone is doing the work, because the two get conflated. Sometimes what looks like a racial pattern is really a geographic one. An offender hunts the area he knows, and in a segregated city that area may be racially homogeneous, so his victims share a race not because he selected for race but because he selected for the neighborhood, and the neighborhood did the sorting for him. Other times the pattern is genuinely cultural: Dahmer's comfort zone was a subculture rather than a district, and his victims reflected who was present in that subculture. The lesson for an investigator is not to assume that a racially consistent victim set proves a racial preference. It may only prove where the offender felt at home.

What the data actually shows

The pattern holds, but it is considerably stronger for some offenders than others, and this is where most popular accounts, including my own earlier version of this talk, have been imprecise.

In the Radford and Florida Gulf Coast University data, 81.9 percent of white serial killers killed only white victims, while among black serial killers, 43.4 percent killed only black victims. Both figures exceed what random victim selection would produce, so the tendency is present in both groups, but as these numbers have it, it is close to twice as strong among white offenders. I offer that comparison with a caveat, and it is an important one: the statistics in this field are not fixed, and not every study agrees on which figures are currently accurate. Different databases define their terms differently, draw from different case populations, and update on different schedules, and a number that looks authoritative in one report will be revised in the next. What is stable across the sources is the direction of the finding, that offenders tend to kill within their own group. What varies is the precise strength, and anyone who tells you the exact percentage is settled is overstating what the data can bear.

An investigator should take the practical lesson rather than the tidy one. Victim race is genuine evidence about an offender, and it is stronger evidence in some circumstances than in others. Treating it as a hard constraint will cost you cases.

What that looks like in practice is not what most readers assume. An investigator does not treat victim demographics as a prediction of the offender's demographics. He treats them as evidence about where the offender was able to move unnoticed, which is a different and more useful claim. A series of victims from one neighborhood or one demographic group tells you the offender had access to that neighborhood or that group, and had reason to be there without generating alarm. It does not tell you he shared the demographics of his victims. Very often he did, because access follows familiarity, but the direction of the inference matters: the evidence points at his comfort zone first and at his identity only through it. Combined with what the geography, the signature, and the trophies say, victim demographics become one of the constraints from Chapter 1 - narrowing the population of possible offenders without ever naming one, until the remainder is small enough to investigate. Treated alone, it is thin. Combined with the other three pillars, it is what turns a general model of an offender into a workable one.

The composition of offenders has shifted

Two related numbers are worth putting on the page, because they are frequently asserted without any figures attached and they have changed substantially over time.

Across the full historical record, U.S. serial killers are 53.3 percent white, 39.3 percent black, 5.6 percent Hispanic, and small percentages Asian and Native American. But that aggregate conceals a steep trend. In the 1920s, black offenders were 17.9 percent of the total. By the 1990s the figure was 43.5 percent, by the 2000s 54.2 percent, and in the 2010s 55.2 percent. The proportion has risen in nearly every decade since the 1920s, and for the last three decades of data, black offenders have been the majority.

Victims track population figures closely, with one clear exception. White victims are roughly 66 percent of the total against a white share of the population near 62 percent. Black victims are roughly 27 percent against a black share of the population near 13 percent, which is to say black Americans are victimized at about twice their share of the population.

I am going to state those numbers and decline to explain them, and I want to be direct about why rather than appearing to dodge. Explaining that trend would require a serious treatment of urbanization, policing patterns, which homicides get investigated thoroughly and which do not, how missing persons are classified, and which cases become known cases in the first place. Those are real questions with real literatures behind them, and none of them are mine. What I can tell you is what an investigator does with the numbers, which is to treat victim demographics as evidence about an offender's comfort zone, and nothing more than that.

How the Four Work Together

No single pillar links a case. In practice, the pillars corroborate each other, and the pattern is recognizable well before any one of them is conclusive.

Consider what a linkage argument actually looks like when it is put in front of a supervisor or, later, a jury. Two victims from the same demographic group. Two scenes inside a bounded area that shares an anchor. One unnecessary behavior that appears at both, which serves no purpose in accomplishing either crime. Something missing from both scenes that a robbery would not explain. Each of those observations is weak alone. Together, and this is the actual arithmetic of the job, they constrain the population of possible offenders down to a size an investigation can work with.

Which raises the more interesting question of how the pillars interact, because they do not carry equal weight in every case and they do not always agree.

In practice the pillars fall into two natural pairs. The first pair - comfort zone and victim demographics - is about access. They answer the question of who the offender could get near without being noticed. The second pair - signature and trophies - is about the offender himself. They answer the question of what he needed to do that the crime did not require, and what he could not bear to leave behind. An investigation ideally has evidence in both pairs, because the pairs constrain in different directions. Access tells you the population he was drawing from. Signature and trophies tell you which offender inside that population you are looking at.

When the pairs agree, the linkage argument writes itself. Two scenes inside a bounded geographic area, victims from the same demographic group, the same unnecessary ritual detail at both, and a category of object missing from both that a robbery would not explain - that is not one weak claim about a single offender; it is four independent narrow claims that all point at the same person. A defense attorney can attack any one of them. She cannot easily attack all four at once, because each rests on a different kind of evidence.

When the pairs disagree is where the interesting cases live. A tightly bounded geography and consistent victim demographics, with no recognizable signature and no missing objects: the offender may be careful in ways that are frustrating the linkage tools rather than absent from them, or the cases may not, in fact, belong together. A distinctive signature repeating across scenes spread across the country, with no coherent comfort zone and no consistent victim group: the mobility itself is the story, and the next chapter spends time with the two cases where that happened. Neither of those patterns proves the linkage is wrong. Each of them tells you what the investigation needs to do next, because it names which pillar is doing the work and which one is failing to.

The pillars are not four inputs to a formula. They are four categories of evidence that answer slightly different questions, and the skill of reading them is not adding them up but understanding what each of them is telling you when they agree and, more importantly, when they do not.

Note also what the four pillars have in common. Not one of them requires a theory of the offender's mind. Where he was comfortable, what he could not help doing, what he could not leave behind, and who he could approach without being noticed are all inferences from physical evidence and case records. You can build every one of them without ever asking why.

That is the methodology. The next chapter puts it against real cases, including several where it worked and at least one where it did not.

ON THE RECORD

Established

- **Comfort zones and anchor points.** Offenders operate where they are unremarkable, usually near a residence or workplace, and the anchor is not always geographic; it can be a subculture or a setting.
- **Signature versus modus operandi.** M.O. is learned method and changes over time, so it is a weak basis for linking cases. A signature is an unnecessary ritual that serves the offender, and it is the stronger link, but it is only visible once it recurs.
- **Trophies.** Offenders keep personal items far more often than cash, and those kept objects are frequently what ties a suspect to multiple cases once a search warrant is served.
- **Racial and cultural barriers.** Offenders tend to kill within their own group, chiefly because that is where they move without being

noticed. Sometimes an apparent racial pattern is really just the geography of a segregated hunting ground.

Myth

- **That signature and M.O.** are the same thing. Conflating them is the most consequential terminology error in the field, and it leads investigators to link cases on method alone.
- **That collecting body parts is common.** It is not. The common trophy is ordinary: clothing, jewelry, a personal effect.

Still unsettled

- **The precise strength of the racial-barrier pattern.** The direction is stable across studies; the exact figures are not, and different databases disagree on the current numbers.
- **Why victim demographics fall as they do.** The overrepresentation of some groups among victims involves questions of policing, classification, and which cases become known cases at all, which are outside this book's lane.

How the four work together

- **The pillars fall into two pairs.** Comfort zone and victim demographics tell you who the offender could reach unnoticed; signature and trophies tell you which offender inside that population you are looking at. Linkage is strongest when the pairs agree and most informative about the case when they do not.

Chapter 5: Weapons and Method - Capability and Access

The four pillars are about behavior at the scene. Where the offender was comfortable, what he could not stop doing, what he could not bear to leave behind, and who he was able to approach without being noticed - all four are questions an investigator answers by reading what a body and a location say to him after the offender is gone.

There is a fifth question that precedes all of them, and it belongs on its own because it is answered before the offender ever gets to the scene. What did he do it with?

Method choice is not a new pillar. It sits underneath Pillar Two, alongside signature and modus operandi, and it operates by the same logic - an offender chooses what he uses, and the choice reveals something about him whether he intended it to or not. But method is worth its own chapter, because two very different things get read from it and the two are constantly confused. The first is what the offender was capable of. The second is what was available to him. Those are not the same question, and treating them as one is how the evil-genius myth from Chapter 3 gets built, and how it gets refuted less often than it should.

This chapter separates them.

Capability

Return to the IQ table from Chapter 3. It looked at first like a table about intelligence. It is really a table about distance.

The Radford and Florida Gulf Coast University database recorded IQ scores for 323 serial killers. The average is 92.7, the median 85, and the standard deviation is 24.4 - far wider than the population's 15, for a reason the database is candid about and I will come to. Below is the average IQ for each recorded method, along with N, meaning the number of offenders each average is based on. That number matters here, because some of the rows rest on very few people:

Method	Average IQ	N
Bomb	130.7	3
Strangle / Shoot	105.6	8
Poison	100.0	1
Strangle / Bludgeon	99.6	10
Strangle	94.4	46
Stab	93.4	28
Stab / Shoot	93.2	33
Stab / Strangle	91.5	18
Shoot	89.3	76
Bludgeon / Shoot	86.6	13
Bludgeon / Stab	85.4	12
Bludgeon	84.2	15

Read down the column and one relationship stands out. The methods that put distance between the offender and the victim cluster at the top. The methods that require the offender to be within arm's reach cluster at the bottom. Bombs and the compound remote methods sit above the mean; single-implement, close-contact methods sit below. Intelligence, in these numbers, is tracking how far from the victim the offender is willing or able to be.

Bombers score highest by a wide margin, and the reason is not mysterious: building a functioning explosive device that works when it is supposed to, and does not detonate in your own hands first, requires technical competence that most people simply do not have. Ted Kaczynski, the Unabomber, held a doctorate in mathematics from the University of Michigan and had held an assistant professorship at Berkeley before he moved to a cabin in Montana.

Kaczynski is worth pausing on, because he is a useful edge case rather than a clean example. Over seventeen years he built and delivered sixteen bombs, and they killed three people. He is famous, and he is frequently cited in exactly this context, but by the raw arithmetic of victims he barely satisfies the definition of a serial killer at all. What made him extraordinarily hard to catch was not a high body count. It was his method. He killed remotely. He mailed or planted his devices and was nowhere near them when they went off, which means he left almost none of the evidence that the rest of this book is about. No comfort zone in the usual sense, no scene he was present at, no victim who ever saw him. The bomb category scores highest on intelligence precisely because remote, technical killing selects for the small number of offenders who can manage it, and that same remoteness is what makes those offenders the exception to nearly every method in these pages.

At the other end, offenders who bludgeon average 84.2, which is below the group mean and more than ten points below the population average of 100. That also fits. Bludgeoning requires no planning, no acquisition, no skill, and no tool that is not already in the room.

One caution about that table, and it applies to a great deal of the data in this book. Those averages are drawn from very different sample sizes, which is why the N column is printed alongside them. The bomb figure rests on three people. The poison figure rests on one. The shoot and strangle figures rest on dozens. A mean built from three cases would move several points if two more offenders were added; a mean built from seventy-six is stable. I flag this because the top-line numbers are often quoted without it, and a mean built from a handful of cases is a weaker claim than a mean built from tens. The direction of the finding is solid. The precision implied by a figure like 130.7 is not.

There is one more caution the database itself insists on, and it is worth passing along because it cuts against over-reading any single figure. The IQ scores in the database are not a random sample. An offender's IQ tends to get reported publicly when it is unusually high or unusually low - a genius-level score makes headlines, and a score below 70 becomes a live issue in a death-penalty case, because it is unconstitutional to execute someone below that line. Scores in the ordinary middle rarely get published at all. That reporting bias is why the spread in this data is so wide, and it is another reason to trust the shape of the table over the exact value in any one cell.

There is more to say about method as evidence, and this chapter is not the place to say it. What the IQ table hints at is that method choice encodes something about the offender's capability, and capability is only half of the story. The other half is what he could get his hands on.

Access

Capability is what the offender can do. Access is what is available to him. These are constantly conflated, and the conflation runs in the direction the evil-genius myth wants: an unusual method looks like an unusual mind, when very often it just means an unusual environment.

Consider a period the popular literature almost never covers. From roughly 1780 to 1810, the frontier that would eventually become the United States produced a substantial number of what a modern eye would recognize as serial homicides. Samuel Mason, mentioned briefly in Chapter 2, ran a river-piracy series from 1797 to 1803 and killed an uncertain number of travelers along the Ohio and Mississippi. The Harpe brothers, also from Chapter 2, killed across the same frontier over four years in the 1790s and were prolific enough that the Library of Congress records their series as among the first documented in American history.

A modern reader who knows the method statistics from the Radford table will notice something. These offenders did not shoot their victims, or not usually. They did not strangle them. The weapon of choice across the frontier period was the axe - the hand-axe, the belt-axe, the tomahawk, whichever version the offender was carrying - because that was the tool every man on the frontier already owned. A firearm in 1795 was an expensive, temperamental, slow object to reload. An axe was on the offender's belt because he needed one for the ordinary work of being alive that week.

The observation I want to draw from this is one my outline says I should flag as such, so I will. This is my read, not the record. I have not seen a systematic peer-reviewed cross-tabulation of serial-murder method by decade or region that separates availability from other factors, and the frontier data is thin enough that any strong claim about it is doing more with less than I am comfortable with. What I am confident about is the logic. Weapon choice tracks era and environment as much as it tracks anything about the offender's mind. A man in 1795 who reached for the tool on his belt was not making a statement about his intellect. He was using what was available and unremarkable in his world.

Across Borders

The historical version of this argument is thin on documentation, as I have already flagged. The modern cross-border version is not.

The Radford and Florida Gulf Coast University Serial Killer Database records the method used by every offender in its files, and it separates U.S. offenders from those in the rest of the world. The comparison is stark. Here are the single-method categories that account for the bulk of serial homicide, U.S. against international, from Table 13.01 of the 2023 annual report:

Method	U.S.	International
Shoot	36.7%	13.1%
Strangle	9.7%	18.6%
Stab	6.9%	15.1%
Poison	3.8%	11.8%
Bludgeon	4.2%	10.5%

Read the two columns together. American serial killers shoot at nearly three times the international rate. Every other method - strangulation, stabbing, poison, bludgeoning - runs roughly twice as often outside the U.S. as inside it. Multiple-method offenders, ones who used more than one weapon across their series, also skew American: 36.8 percent of U.S. offenders versus 26.8 percent internationally. The pattern is not subtle, and it is not what most readers expect.

Before drawing any argument from it, I want to close off a reading of this data that is available on the surface and is wrong on the substance. A reader who looks at that first row and concludes that American firearm availability inflates the number of serial murders is misreading the table. The columns are method distributions among identified offenders. They are not incidence rates. They tell you what the offenders in each group are doing, not how many offenders there are.

The incidence question has its own data, from earlier in the same report. U.S. offender counts rose through the twentieth century, peaked in the 1980s at 840 for the decade, and have fallen every decade since. International counts, excluding Canada, rose on a similar curve, peaked in the 1990s at 441, and have fallen in every decade since as well. Two very different weapon environments, two curves with the same shape, offset by one decade. Whatever forces have driven the rise and fall of serial murder as a phenomenon, they are not the availability of a particular method, because the phenomenon moved the same direction in places where the particular method was not available.

This is not an argument about firearm policy, and this book will not make one. What the international comparison does is close off a specific misreading of the American data. Availability shapes how, not how much. When one method becomes universally available in a country, offenders in that country will use it. When it is not available elsewhere, offenders elsewhere will use whatever is available - and the international column shows what that looks like in aggregate. Strangulation and stabbing and poison and bludgeoning are all more common in the countries where a firearm is harder to obtain, which is precisely the availability logic this chapter has been building. It runs across borders the same way the frontier-axe read suggested it runs across centuries. The evidence for the cross-border version is documented in a peer-reviewed database. The evidence for the historical version is not, and I have already said so.

One forensic note worth making, because it belongs in a methodology book and not a policy one: the firearm-shifted American distribution is, in an operational sense, easier to work than the international distribution. A bullet leaves a projectile with characteristic striations. A shell casing leaves a firing-pin impression and extractor marks. Both feed into the National Integrated Ballistics Identification Network, or NIBIN, and both can link a weapon to multiple scenes across jurisdictions in a way that a length of cord and a set of manual injuries cannot. Ballistics is one of the most mature forensic disciplines the field has. A poisoning, by contrast, may not be recognized as a homicide at all if the substance is well selected and the offender has any medical plausibility. A strangulation without a distinctive ligature leaves fewer transferable characteristics than a fired round. This does not mean American cases are easier to solve overall - the volume is higher, and the offender pool is larger - but it does mean that when a firearm is used, the evidence it generates is unusually amenable to linkage, which is exactly the question this book has been asking since Chapter 1.

Two cautions belong here before the section closes.

The first is that the international column of that table is almost certainly an undercount, and probably substantially. Radford states the limitation directly in Section 4 of its report: a case enters the database only after a specific chain of events has occurred. The murders must be discovered by law enforcement, tied together, and attributed to an identified offender; that offender's name and the victim counts must be publicized in accessible media; and the reporting must eventually reach sources documented in English. In the United States, all of those steps happen most of the time, most quickly, because of a combination of dense law-enforcement infrastructure, aggressive local and national press, and English-language reporting by default. In developing countries, where policing resources are thinner and press coverage is less consistent, the same chain breaks in more places, and offenders who would enter the database if they had operated in the U.S. simply do not enter it. The consequence for the numbers above is that the international column reflects the offenders who cleared all those reporting hurdles, not the actual distribution of serial murder outside the

U.S. The direction of the finding - that non-firearm methods are more common where firearms are less available - I regard as defensible. The specific magnitudes I do not, and neither should the reader.

The second is that "international" in that table is a single bucket combining Europe, Latin America, Asia, and Africa into one column, and the reader should notice that. A serial killer in Japan and a serial killer in Colombia and a serial killer in Kenya are operating in very different weapon environments, media environments, and law-enforcement environments. Averaging them together produces a number that answers a coarse question well - is the American pattern different from everywhere else? - and answers a finer question badly. A properly stratified international comparison would separate high-income democracies from the rest and would separate the rest by region. Radford's data supports that separation for individual countries with enough cases; the 2023 report does not run the analysis. Anyone doing serious comparative work on serial-murder method would need to.

Same argument as the frontier axe, then, in a form that survives contact with the data. Availability shapes method. Method reveals environment more than mind. The honest historical version of this argument is still waiting to be done systematically, and I am not the person to do it. The honest cross-border version is documented, and it says exactly what the availability logic predicts.

The same principle runs forward. Firearms in twenty-first-century America are so ubiquitous, so cheap, and so socially embedded that a shooting reveals almost nothing about the offender's capability or access. The shoot cell in the Radford IQ table is the largest one, at N=76, with an average IQ of 89.3 - near the group mean, slightly below the population average. That number is not telling you that shooters are unintelligent. It is telling you that when you make a method available to everyone, the offenders who use it will look like everyone. The signal drops out because the availability is universal.

A poisoning in the same environment tells you the opposite. Most Americans do not have easy access to a lethal quantity of any well-selected poison. Buying one draws attention. Manufacturing one requires knowledge most people do not have. Having a legitimate reason to be near one - access through pharmacy, healthcare, chemistry, agriculture, veterinary work - is a much smaller category. A poisoning in the present day is a choice against the grain of availability, and choices against the grain of availability carry more information than choices with it.

That framing - availability as evidence - parallels the comfort-zone logic of Pillar One more closely than it parallels the IQ column. A comfort zone tells you where the offender could be without being noticed. Availability tells you what tools he could obtain without being noticed. Both are constraints on the population of possible offenders, and both work by identifying the smaller subset that had the access rather than by identifying the offender directly. An unusual weapon is like an unusual anchor point. It says: whoever did this had reach into a category most people do not.

This is where a comparison the outline has been pointing at earns its place, because the argument about access takes a specific shape when the data is sorted by sex.

The Radford and Florida Gulf Coast University Serial Killer Database, in its 2023 annual report, records that women serial killers use poison in approximately 54.5 percent of their cases. Men use poison in approximately 2.4 percent of theirs. That is not a small difference. It is a factor of twenty-plus, on a sample large enough to be robust, and it is the single largest method disparity in the sex-difference data. Chapter 8 does the full work of that finding, because it belongs there. But I plant it here for the same reason the outline wants it planted here: poison is the woman-killer's version of what Kaczynski's bomb was. Both are methods that keep the offender absent at the moment of death.

Notice what that structural parallel says, and what it does not say. It does not say that women serial killers are more intelligent than men. The IQ data for that claim does not exist at any sample size worth quoting; the one poison case in the cross-tabulation is one case, and it means nothing. What the parallel says is that the same behavioral logic is at work - a method that requires planning, that does not require physical dominance, that puts distance between offender and victim, and that requires access most people do not have. When a poison is used, the offender was not present when the death occurred. The evidence at the scene is thin the same way it was thin at every Unabomber scene. And the pattern of who uses that method is not evenly distributed across the population, because access to poison is not evenly distributed either, and because the physical dynamics that make some methods practical for one offender and impractical for another sort in a particular direction.

Chapter 8 is the chapter where all of that gets worked through against cases and against the objection that the female-offender data is systematically undercounted. For this chapter, the point that belongs here is the one about access, and it is smaller than the one Chapter 8 will make. Method choice tells an investigator what environment the offender moved through and what tools were reachable inside that environment. The offender who reaches for what is on the frontier belt in 1795, and the offender who reaches for what is in the medicine cabinet today, and the offender who reaches for what is behind the counter at the pharmacy where she works - all three are making choices that reveal an environment more than a mind. Access is a constraint, and constraints narrow the population of possible offenders in exactly the way the four pillars do.

The frontier axe and the modern poison are the same argument, told two centuries apart.

Reading Method as Evidence

Method choice, treated the way this chapter has treated it, answers a two-part question about an offender. What did he have to do? What did he choose to be able to do? The first speaks to necessity - the M.O., the practical steps of accomplishing this particular crime against this particular victim. The second speaks to preparation - what capability he brought, what access he cultivated, what environment he operated inside.

Those two questions are not new questions. They are the same ones the pillars ask, running through a different piece of evidence. Method is not a fifth pillar. It is a signal about the pillars themselves, and reading it well requires holding onto the distinctions the pillars established.

A distinctive weapon may be a signature, if using it is unnecessary for the crime and the offender uses it anyway. It may be an M.O., if it is simply what worked in this environment. Same object, opposite sides of the line - which is the Douglas distinction from Chapter 4, applied one layer down, to the weapon rather than to the ritual. The question is whether the choice served the crime or served the offender, and answering it requires the same discipline of asking, weapon by weapon, which was true here.

A remote method may reflect capability, or it may reflect access, or it may reflect both. Kaczynski had both - a doctorate in mathematics and the reclusive lifestyle that gave him time and space to build. A caregiver who has been at a hospital for fifteen years has access without any particular capability, in the ordinary sense; the technical skill is the medical training that is her professional qualification, and the method is a small increment on top of that. A twentieth-century arsenic case in a rural community may reflect neither capability nor sophistication, but simply the fact that arsenic was in every hardware store as a rat killer for the first half of the century, and using it required nothing more than opening the tin.

These are distinct patterns and they belong distinguished. When method choice is doing multiple kinds of work at once - capability, access, signature, M.O. - the investigator's job is to sort them, not to average them together into a single impression of the offender.

That is the discipline this chapter has been building toward, and it is also the discipline the next chapter will test.

The four pillars, augmented by method as a fifth kind of evidence, describe a methodology that works on most cases most of the time. The next chapter is about the cases where the methodology has to bend, because the offender broke one of the pillars while remaining bound to the others. Ted

Bundy broke the comfort zone by killing across seven states. Dennis Rader, BTK, broke the ordinary logic of stopping, going quiet for over a decade and then not being caught until he restarted the correspondence himself. Both are famous cases. Both are exceptions. Neither dissolves the framework; each of them shows what happens when one pillar fails and the others have to do the work.

Before we get to those two, one thing is worth saying about how method fits in. Bundy used a variety of methods across his series, and shifted between them, which is precisely what the M.O.-changes-over-time rule from Chapter 4 predicts. BTK developed a stable, elaborate method-plus-signature that stayed consistent across a long enough series that the linkage was visible from within the cases themselves. One offender broke geography and let method drift. The other stayed home and let method calcify. Different exceptions. Same framework showing them for what they were.

That is the methodology. The next chapter puts it against the two cases that most tested it.

ON THE RECORD

Established

- **Capability tracks with method, and method tracks with distance from the victim.** The high end of the IQ-by-method table is not smart offenders in the ordinary sense; it is offenders who successfully removed themselves from their own crimes. Remote methods select for the small population that can execute them.

- **Access tracks with era and environment, not with mind.** Weapon choice reflects what was ordinary and available in the offender's world. A frontier hand-axe, a modern firearm, and a hospital medication cabinet are all instances of the same principle: offenders reach for what is unremarkable in their environment.

- **The cross-border data confirms the availability logic.** U.S. serial killers shoot at nearly three times the international rate; every close-contact method runs roughly twice as often outside the U.S. as inside it. Method distribution shifts with availability, but offender counts move on parallel trajectories - availability shapes how, not how much.

- **Method is not a fifth pillar; it is a signal about the pillars.** A distinctive weapon may be signature or M.O.; a remote method may reflect capability or access; the discipline is separating them rather than averaging them together.
- **Poison and bomb are the same structural move.** Both keep the offender absent at the moment of death. The population that selects each is different, but the behavioral logic is identical, and Chapter 8 develops the sex-difference version of it.

Myth

- **That an unusual method reflects an unusual mind.** It usually reflects unusual capability or unusual access, which are different questions and answered differently.
- **That the top of the IQ-by-method table is what serial killers look like.** The top rests on very small Ns, and the bulk of the table sits at or below population average. Reading the top row as typical produces the evil-genius picture and misses the offender who is standing in front of you.

Still unsettled

- **Whether the historical method-by-availability pattern holds up systematically.** My frontier-axe read is a read, not a peer-reviewed cross-tabulation; the direction is defensible, the specifics are not documented at the level the IQ column is.
- **Why the poison sex-difference takes the shape it does.** The disparity is real and robust. Whether it reflects access, planning style, physical dynamics, or a combination has not been separated cleanly in the literature that I know of, and Chapter 8 treats it with appropriate care.

Chapter 6: The Mobility and Signature Exceptions

The four pillars are patterns, not laws. That distinction matters more than it might seem, because a reader who takes them as laws will make exactly the error this chapter is designed to prevent. The way to understand a pattern is to study where it breaks, and the two most famous serial killers in American memory are famous, in part, precisely because each one breaks one of the pillars we have just spent a chapter building.

Ted Bundy broke the comfort zone. He killed across seven states, which is close to the last thing the geography of serial murder predicts. Dennis Rader, BTK, broke the ordinary logic of the signature. Where most signatures are private, involuntary, and something the offender would rather you never noticed, Rader built his deliberately and then spent decades trying to make sure it was seen.

These are the cases everyone knows. They are also, and this is the point of putting them together here, the exceptions that establish the rule rather than dissolving it. Each one is exceptional in a specific, bounded way, and understanding exactly how each one is exceptional teaches the pillar better than a conforming case would. A rule you have only ever seen obeyed is a rule you do not fully understand. You learn what the comfort zone is by watching what it costs Bundy to operate without one, and you learn what a signature is by watching Rader do the opposite of what signatures normally do.

So this chapter closes the loop on the methodology. After it, the book moves into cases that illustrate the pillars rather than test them. But first, the two that test them.

Ted Bundy and the Cost of Mobility

Bundy is the name people reach for whenever they want to argue that the comfort zone is a myth. He killed in Washington, Utah, Colorado, Idaho, Oregon, California, and Florida. At least thirty homicides, spread across a good portion of the American West and then, at the end, the Southeast. If the rule is that serial killers stay close to an anchor point, Bundy looks like the counterexample that breaks it.

He does not break it. He explains it, and he explains it better than any conforming case could, because his mobility was not the freedom it appears to be. It was a symptom of a system coming apart, and the closer you look at when and why he moved, the more clearly the comfort zone reasserts itself underneath the travel.

The early killings were local

Start at the beginning rather than the end, because the beginning is where the pattern is intact. Bundy's first known series was in the Pacific Northwest, around Seattle and then around Salt Lake City after he moved there for law school. Those were anchor points in the textbook sense: places he lived, places he knew, places where he was a resident with a reason to be present and a mental map of the terrain. He abducted women from environments he understood, university areas mostly, and he used approaches that depended on local familiarity. In the phase of his life when he was operating as a free man with a fixed address, Bundy hunted his comfort zone like almost everyone else in this book.

That is the part the popular image leaves out. The cross-country Bundy, the one who seems to disprove the geography, is the late Bundy. The early Bundy, the one who was actually building and sustaining a series, stayed home.

Bundy's first known series was in Washington State, in 1974. His victims that year were college-age women taken from areas around the University of Washington in Seattle, from Central Washington State College in Ellensburg, and from Oregon State University in Corvallis, all inside a corridor Bundy knew personally. He was a law student and a Republican Party volunteer with a Seattle address. His girlfriend at the time lived in the same city. His mother lived within an easy drive. Every one of the eight Washington and Oregon victims that year was taken within a defined region he had a legitimate reason to move through.

Two of the abductions on July 14, 1974, from Lake Sammamish State Park east of Seattle, were witnessed. Multiple people that day saw a young man with his arm in a fake sling, driving a light Volkswagen Beetle, approaching young women and asking for help carrying something to his car. Two women, Janice Ott and Denise Naslund, disappeared from the park that afternoon within a few hours of each other. The description of the man, the sling ruse, and the Beetle were consistent across witnesses. What the Lake Sammamish witnesses were describing was not a stranger from elsewhere. They were describing an offender who was comfortable enough at that specific state park on that specific Sunday to work it in daylight, twice.

That is the anchor in operation. The comfort zone is not a myth Bundy broke. It is a well-documented feature of his early career, on the day he was arguably closest to being caught if anyone had been looking for the pattern.

He moved to Utah in the autumn of 1974 to attend law school, and the killings moved with him. His Utah victims were taken from within his new corridor: Salt Lake City, Bountiful, Murray. When he was arrested in Salt Lake City in August 1975 on suspicion of an attempted kidnapping, a search of his vehicle turned up a crowbar, an ice pick, handcuffs, garbage bags, and a ski mask with eye holes cut in it. He was a resident of the area. His girlfriend from Seattle had followed him there. He had again constructed a comfort zone, and again he had worked inside it.

The travel was flight, not hunting

What changed was that he got caught.

Bundy was arrested, and then he escaped, and then he was arrested again, and then he escaped again. His famous geographic range, the part that lands him in every discussion of the traveling killer, largely happened during and after those escapes. The Colorado killings, the flight to Florida, the final murders there: these were the actions of a fugitive who could not go home because home was where the police were waiting, not the actions of a killer who had transcended the need for a comfort zone.

This is a crucial distinction, and it is the reason Bundy belongs in a chapter about the pillar rather than a chapter dismissing it. There is a difference between an offender who ranges widely because that is how he prefers to operate and an offender who ranges widely because staying put would get him arrested. The first would genuinely contradict the comfort zone principle. The second confirms it from the outside, by showing what happens when a killer is forcibly separated from his anchor point. Bundy on the run was not a more evolved predator. He was a less effective one, improvising in unfamiliar territory, and it showed.

Florida shows the cost

The Florida murders are the tell. By the time Bundy reached Florida, he was operating with none of the advantages his early crimes had. He did not know the ground. He had no stable identity in place, no established routine to hide inside, no mental map of which spaces were watched and which were not. He was a stranger, which is precisely the condition the comfort zone exists to avoid.

Two weeks after arriving in Tallahassee, on the night of January 15, he entered the Chi Omega sorority house at Florida State University in the early morning hours and attacked four women in approximately fifteen minutes. Two of them, Margaret Bowman and Lisa Levy, were killed. Two survived. Another survivor was attacked at a nearby residence a short time later.

This is nothing like the Bundy of Washington State. The Chi Omega attack was fast, chaotic, and public. He entered a residence he had not surveilled, containing sleeping occupants he had not selected, and did his work in a compressed window before fleeing on foot. Nita Neary, a resident of the house, saw him leaving. She would later provide the description that connected him to the scene. There was no ruse, no approach, no manipulation of the sort he had used with such calm at Lake Sammamish. There was violence in an unfamiliar space, at speed, and it left behind exactly the evidence the earlier crimes had been careful not to.

Three weeks later, on February 9, 1978, Bundy abducted twelve-year-old Kimberly Leach from her middle school in Lake City, Florida, in daylight, and was seen doing so. He was a stranger in the town. He drove a stolen white van. Multiple witnesses saw the van, the man, and the girl together. He was arrested within a week.

And the Florida crimes were, by comparison to his earlier ones, chaotic. Where the Northwest killings had shown planning and control, the attack at the Chi Omega sorority house was frenzied and left him badly exposed. He was operating outside his zone, under pressure, and the work degraded accordingly. It was in Florida, out of his territory, that the evidence finally accumulated to the point of a conviction that stuck, including the bite-mark evidence that helped tie him to the sorority attack.

Read that way, Bundy is not the exception to the comfort zone. He is the experiment that proves it, a controlled demonstration of what happens to a serial killer's effectiveness when you strip his anchor point away. He got sloppy the moment he left home. Most of them would.

What Bundy actually was the exception to

If Bundy conforms to the geography once you account for the escapes, it is worth being honest about what he genuinely was exceptional at, because he was exceptional, and pretending otherwise overcorrects.

Bundy was atypical in his presentation. Articulate, educated, conventionally presentable, enrolled in law school, capable of putting a stranger at ease long enough to get her within reach. That is the real Bundy exception, and it maps onto a different part of this book: the myth of the evil genius from Chapter 3, and the availability-vulnerability-desirability framework from Chapter 2. Bundy's gift was not geographic range. It was social access. He could approach victims that a more obviously threatening man could not, because he did not read as a threat. His charm was his method, in the modus operandi sense, and it was effective enough that he did not need to overpower his way to a victim when he could talk his way there instead.

But social access is not the same thing as geographic freedom, and conflating the two is how Bundy became the patron saint of the traveling-killer myth. He moved widely because he was fleeing, and he charmed widely because that was his approach. The first was forced on him. The second was his talent. Only the second was genuinely rare.

A note on the bite marks

The bite-mark evidence deserves a closer look, because I have spent a good deal of my career photographing bite marks, and the Bundy case sits at a revealing point in that history.

Bite marks are among the most difficult injuries to document well, and the difficulty is a matter of timing and biology. By the time a victim reaches a studio for proper photography, or by the time a body is examined, the mark has usually changed. Bruising spreads and darkens, the crisp indentations left by individual teeth soften, and the pattern that was sharp at the moment of injury has begun to blur into a diffuse contusion. What the camera captures a day later is often a shadow of what was there at the start.

The techniques for dealing with that problem were, in the late nineteen seventies, extremely new. The first American court acceptance of bite-mark evidence came in a California case in 1975. Bundy's Florida trial was in 1979. So when that evidence helped convict him, the entire practice of presenting bite marks in an American courtroom was four years old. It was frontier science, and it was treated with a confidence that, in hindsight, the underlying discipline had not yet earned.

That distinction matters, and I want to be precise about it, because two different things get lumped together under the phrase bite-mark evidence. One is the photographic documentation of the injury, which is my area, and which has genuinely advanced. Modern practice can call on ultraviolet imaging, which brings out surface bruising and faint early patterns by making them fluoresce, and infrared imaging, which penetrates deeper and can render subdermal bruising and pressure patterns that faded from view in ordinary light. The standards body I served on addressed infrared photography of bruising and patterned injuries directly. Those imaging methods are real improvements, and they are largely confined to laboratory settings rather than the field, because they require control over ambient light that a crime scene does not offer.

The other thing is bite-mark comparison: the claim that a mark on a body can be matched to a particular suspect's dentition with the confidence of a fingerprint. That claim has not held up. In the decades since Bundy, forensic odontology's comparison side has been substantially discredited, undone by proficiency studies showing that examiners could not reliably agree even on whether a given mark was a human bite, let alone whose. Documenting the injury accurately is a solvable technical problem. Matching it to one person's teeth, to the standard a courtroom was told to expect, turned out not to be.

So Bundy is a marker in two timelines at once. He sits near the beginning of bite-mark evidence's rise, convicted partly on a technique in its infancy, and he sits well before its fall. I document these injuries for a living and I take the documentation seriously. That is exactly why I am careful to separate the photograph, which can be done well, from the comparison, which for years was presented as more certain than it ever was.

That is the seam this section wants to open, because Bundy sits near the beginning of a much longer story about what happened to bite-mark comparison in the decades after his execution.

In February 2009, the National Academy of Sciences released a report titled Strengthening Forensic Science in the United States. It was the most comprehensive review of forensic-science reliability in American history, commissioned by Congress, and it was devastating. On bite-mark comparison specifically, the report found no scientific basis for the discipline's core individualization claim - that a bite mark on human skin could be matched to a specific set of teeth with any reasonable degree of certainty. The report concluded that the discipline had never established either the uniqueness of human dentition or the fidelity of transfer from teeth to skin, and that examiner conclusions on bite marks were being introduced in criminal trials without meaningful scientific validation.

Every major body to review the evidence since has confirmed the finding. The President's Council of Advisors on Science and Technology reached the same conclusion in 2016. The Texas Forensic Science Commission recommended a moratorium the same year. The National Institute of Standards and Technology's 2022 report on bitemark analysis was the fourth major scientific body to find no scientific validity supporting the discipline's central claims. The Innocence Project lists more than twenty-five people wrongfully convicted or arrested on the strength of bite-mark evidence who have since been exonerated, several after decades in prison.

Two things need to be said honestly at this point, and they cut in different directions.

The first is that this book is not making an argument that Bundy was wrongly convicted. He was not. The bite-mark evidence at his Chi Omega trial was corroborative rather than dispositive, and the record of what he did in Florida is not in serious dispute. He confessed to over thirty murders before his execution. His conviction stands regardless of what the discipline that helped secure it has since been shown to be worth.

The second is that the story of bite-mark evidence is one of the clearest illustrations in the history of American forensic science of a technique becoming admissible in court, being used in dozens of high-profile cases, and only afterward being subjected to the sort of scientific scrutiny that should have preceded its admissibility in the first place. That is a discipline problem, not a Bundy problem. It is worth naming, in a book about how the evidence at a scene gets read, because the honest answer to the question of how well we read that particular kind of evidence is: less well than the courtroom was told at the time.

Bite-mark comparison, as an individualization technique, should not have been offered in court with the certainty it was offered in the 1970s and 1980s. Photography and documentation of injuries, the demonstrative side of the work I did for a career, is not the problem. Making the images is straightforward, given the right equipment and the discipline to work quickly and consistently. The problem was and remains the interpretation - the step where an examiner looks at a photographed mark and offers a courtroom opinion about which specific person's teeth produced it. That step has never had the scientific foundation the discipline claimed for it, and it should not be treated as if it does now.

BTK and the Manufactured Signature

Dennis Rader gave himself the name. BTK, for bind, torture, kill, was his own coinage, submitted to the police and the press because he wanted the series to have a name and did not trust anyone else to give it the right one. That single fact tells you almost everything about how he inverts the pillar.

Who actually names the killer

Before we get to Rader, it is worth asking where the self-naming serial killer comes from, because most people would answer with the wrong case. The popular assumption is that this began with Jack the Ripper, the original signature killer, who taunted the police with letters and gave himself his famous name. It is a clean origin story, and it is almost certainly not true.

The name Jack the Ripper comes from a letter, the one addressed to Dear Boss and signed with that name, sent to a London news agency in 1888. But the weight of expert opinion, including the researchers who have examined all two hundred-odd letters attributed to the Ripper, is that the murderer wrote none of them, and that Dear Boss in particular was very likely the work of a journalist. This was the era of the sensational press, of newspapers competing for a terrified public's pennies, and a serial murderer without a face or a name is a harder story to sell across weeks of coverage than one with a catchy byline and a personal grudge. So the press, in effect, gave the killer a name and a voice, wrote him a letter in his own hand, and sold the result. The most famous self-naming in the history of serial murder appears to have been a marketing decision made by someone who never killed anyone.

Hold on to that, because it connects directly to the argument of Chapter 3. The signature-as-persona, the killer who brands himself and performs for an audience, was in this foundational case not the offender's doing at all. It was a story told about him, manufactured to sell papers. The public's mental image of what a serial killer does, taunt, name himself, crave the spotlight, traces back to a persona that a newspaper may have invented whole.

The genuine article does exist, though, and the clearest real example predates Rader. The killer who called himself the Zodiac, active in Northern California in the late nineteen sixties and early seventies, wrote more than twenty letters to police and the press, and the name was his own. "This is the Zodiac speaking" was how he opened his communications, and unlike the Ripper letters, the authorship is not seriously in doubt. The Zodiac wanted an audience, demanded that his letters be published under threat of further killing, and built cryptograms specifically to be solved by the public. He is the real thing that the Ripper legend only imitated in advance: a killer who genuinely made himself into a character.

There is a third way a killer gets his name, and it is the one closest to my own experience, so I will only sketch it here and return to it later in the book. Sometimes the name is imposed by others, and imposed wrongly. For most of the nineteen eighties, a string of murders of women in South Los Angeles was attributed to a single figure the press and police called the

Southside Slayer, believed at various points to be responsible for twenty, forty, even fifty killings across the county. He did not exist, at least not as one man. Improved forensics and patient work eventually established that the murders lumped under that one name were the work of several different killers hunting the same population in the same area at the same time. One mythical name had been laid over the crimes of many separate offenders, which is the linkage problem running in reverse: instead of failing to connect one killer's crimes, investigators had wrongly merged many killers into a single phantom.

One of the real men hiding inside that phantom was eventually separated out, and when a journalist rebranded him years later, for a long silence in the middle of his series, she gave him the name the world now knows. That is my case, and its naming has its own chapter. For now it is enough to notice that it represents a fourth category alongside the press-invented Ripper, the self-naming Zodiac, and the recognition-hungry Rader: the killer named by others who were, at first, not even sure how many killers they were naming.

Which brings us, finally, to Rader, who took the authentic version of this behavior further than anyone.

Recall the signature as Chapter 4 defined it. It is a ritual, something the offender does that is not necessary to complete the crime. And critically, in the ordinary case, it is involuntary and private. The offender performs it because he needs to, not because he wants it seen, and frequently he would prefer that no one ever connect the dots. The signature betrays him. It leaks out despite his efforts, and it is most visible on the crimes that went wrong. That is the normal relationship between an offender and his signature: it is a liability he cannot stop producing.

Rader took that relationship and turned it inside out.

A signature performed for an audience

Rader's rituals were real signatures in the technical sense. The binding, the specific ways he controlled and posed his victims, the elements that recurred across scenes and served his own needs rather than the practical demands of the crime: all of that fits the definition exactly. Had he done nothing else, he would be a case study in signature like any other, identifiable across scenes by the ritual that repeated.

But he did do something else. He communicated. He wrote to the police and to newspapers. He sent packages. He described his own crimes, named himself, and complained, in writing, when he felt his work was not being given its due. At one point he asked the police, in effect, how he could get his story out. He wanted credit, and the wanting was not incidental to his psychology; it was central to it. The crimes and the communication about the crimes were part of the same compulsion.

This is the inversion. A normal offender's signature points inward, serving a private need he would rather keep private. Rader's pointed outward. He needed the signature to be witnessed, attributed, and admired, and he took enormous personal risk over decades to make sure it was. The same man who evaded capture from 1974 into the 2000s could not stop reaching out to the very institutions trying to catch him, because being uncaught was not enough for him. He needed to be uncaught and known.

Why the manufactured signature is still a signature

It would be easy to conclude that Rader's need for recognition disqualifies his rituals as true signatures, that a performed signature is something other than a real one. That conclusion is wrong, and the reason it is wrong is instructive.

The binding and posing served Rader's needs, not the crime's. That is the whole test, and it passes regardless of whether he also wanted an audience. What the audience-seeking adds is a second layer of signature on top of the first: the communications themselves became a ritual, recurring, unnecessary to the crime, and unmistakably his. The letters were as much a signature as the binding was. Rader did not replace his signature with performance. He extended it into performance, which gave investigators two categories of recurring, offender-specific behavior to work with instead of one.

From a linkage standpoint, this made Rader simultaneously harder and easier. Harder, because the long silences between communications let the case go cold more than once, and a signature you have to wait years to see again is a signature that does not help you in the interim. Easier, because when he did communicate, he handed investigators material that pointed unambiguously at a single author, and ultimately it was his own outreach, and a traceable piece of digital evidence he assumed was anonymous, that ended the case.

The vanity was the vulnerability

There is a lesson in Rader that generalizes past his particular case, and it is worth stating plainly because it runs against the intuition the fiction has built.

The offender's need to be recognized is not a strength. It is the flaw. Rader stayed free for a very long time on the strength of ordinary caution, and he lost his freedom the moment his caution collided with his vanity. He wanted credit badly enough to keep communicating, and the communication is what caught him. The mastermind of fiction is undone by a brilliant adversary. The real Rader was undone by his own need to be appreciated, which he could not suppress even when suppressing it was the only thing standing between him and a cell.

The Rader case is the paradigm example of this made operational. In 2004, sixteen years after his last known murder, Rader resumed communicating with police and press. Over the course of that year he sent a series of eleven packages containing letters, cryptic word puzzles, and physical evidence - driver's licenses of victims, jewelry, a bound doll wrapped in plastic - to television stations and to the police directly. He was demanding attention on his own terms, and he was getting it.

In January 2005 he sent police a letter asking whether documents on a floppy disk could be traced. This is the sentence that catches me every time I read it, because it is a moment where the offender has exposed his own vulnerability plainly, on paper, in his own words. He wanted to communicate with police using a more efficient medium and he wanted to know whether the medium was safe.

Police, working with a strategy that had been developed for exactly this contingency, placed a message in the Wichita Eagle newspaper telling him it was safe. It was not. A floppy disk that had been used on a personal computer typically retained metadata - user names, license information, deleted-file remnants - that a forensic examiner could recover. The strategy was to lie to him and see whether he took the bait.

He did. On February 16, 2005, he sent a floppy disk to KSAS-TV. Detective Randy Stone of the Wichita Police Department examined it and recovered two pieces of metadata that had survived Rader's attempt to clean the disk. One was a user name: Dennis. The other was a Microsoft Word licensee: Christ Lutheran Church. A web search identified Dennis Rader as the president of the congregation at Christ Lutheran Church in Park City, Kansas. Nine days later, on February 25, DNA obtained from a pap smear of Rader's daughter, retrieved with a warrant from her university's medical clinic, confirmed a familial match to biological evidence recovered from an earlier scene. Rader was arrested that afternoon.

Look at the shape of what just happened. A serial offender who had gone undetected for thirty-one years, and who had gone quiet for the last thirteen of them, was located, identified, and arrested within a matter of weeks - from the moment he asked, on paper, whether he was safe to keep communicating. The floppy disk was the vulnerability. The vanity was what made him send it.

That is the deeper way BTK proves the pillar. A signature is something the offender cannot help producing. Rader is the extreme case, the man whose compulsion to leave and then publicize his signature was so strong that it overrode his considerable instinct for self-preservation. He could not stop, and could not stay quiet, and the not-being-able-to-stop is the entire principle, taken to its logical limit.

Both cases refute a version of the framework that neither offender was actually violating, and both cases illustrate the framework more clearly than a conforming case could have. This is a general feature of exceptions in any evidentiary discipline. The clean cases confirm the rule and teach little; the ambiguous cases test it and teach almost everything worth knowing.

There is a further lesson, which is worth naming because it applies to the case chapters that follow. The pillars are not tests an offender passes or fails. They are patterns visible in the evidence, and a pattern's absence in any given case is not the same as a pattern's disproof. Bundy killed inside a comfort zone until he was jailed twice and could no longer maintain one. Rader stayed home and cultivated a signature so thoroughly that it became the mechanism of his own eventual identification. Both cases, read carefully, are evidence for the pillars rather than against them. This is not a rigged reading. It is the reading the evidence supports when the specific facts of each case are given the weight they deserve, rather than being flattened into the popular versions of the stories.

The case chapters ahead do not require the framework to be tested. They require it to be applied. What Bundy and Rader together establish is that the application is possible, and that when the evidence appears to contradict the pillars it usually does so on a first reading rather than a careful one.

What the Two Exceptions Teach

Put side by side, Bundy and Rader make the same argument from opposite directions.

Bundy appears to break the geography and does not; his mobility was flight, and stripped of his comfort zone he became less effective, not more. Rader appears to break the logic of the signature and does not; his need for recognition did not cancel his signature but doubled it, and the compulsion behind it was so strong it destroyed him. In both cases the pillar holds. In both cases the offender is famous precisely for the feature that looks like an exception, which is why both are so badly misunderstood, and why the fiction built on them is so misleading.

This is also why the two belong together and why they belong here, at the seam between the methodology and the cases. They are the last two chapters' worth of principle, tested at the edges and found intact. Everything after this point is illustration: cases where the pillars operate not at their breaking point but in their ordinary, grinding, effective normal. Starting with an offender whose comfort zone was not a place at all.

ON THE RECORD

Established

- **Bundy confirms the comfort zone rather than breaking it.** His early killings were local and anchored. His cross-country range came during flight after two escapes from custody, and once outside his territory his crimes grew chaotic and exposed him.

- **Bundy's real exception was social, not geographic.** His advantage was access: he could approach victims because he did not read as a threat. That is a victim-selection point, not a mobility one.
- **Rader's signature was real and doubled.** The binding and posing served him, not the crime, which makes them a true signature. His communications became a second signature layer on top of the first.
- **The need for recognition was the flaw.** Rader stayed free on ordinary caution and was undone by his own compulsion to be known. Vanity, not a brilliant adversary, ended the case.

Myth

- **That Bundy proves serial killers roam freely.** He is the most-cited traveling killer and the worst template for the average offender, who stays home.
- **That Jack the Ripper named himself.** The name came from a letter widely believed to be the work of the sensational press, not the murderer. The self-naming killer the public imagines began, in its most famous case, as a newspaper's creation.
- **The spectrum of naming**
- **Killers get their names four different ways.** Invented by the press (Ripper), chosen by the killer himself (Zodiac), demanded through relentless self-promotion (Rader), or imposed by others unsure how many killers they were even naming (the Southside Slayer, later separated into its real offenders).

Chapter 7: The Comfort Zone That Isn't a Map

At around two in the morning on May 27, 1991, two young women on a street corner in Milwaukee found a boy who could not stand up.

He was fourteen years old. His name was Konerak Sinthasomphone, and his family had come to Wisconsin from Laos. He was naked, injured, and unable to speak coherently, and he had just escaped from an apartment in the building behind him. Sandra Smith and her cousin Nicole Childress, who was seventeen, called the police. So did Smith's mother, Glenda Cleveland, who lived nearby.

Three officers responded. So did the man the boy had escaped from.

Jeffrey Dahmer told the officers that the boy was nineteen, that he was Dahmer's boyfriend, and that they had been drinking and had a disagreement. The officers walked with them back to the apartment. They did not run the boy's identification, because there was none. They did not take the names of the two women who had called. Inside the apartment there were no obvious signs of struggle, so they left.

Within the hour, Konerak Sinthasomphone was dead.

Glenda Cleveland called the Department back that night, and again in the days that followed, and again after she saw the boy's photograph in the newspaper under a missing persons notice. She was told there was nothing to it. She called the FBI. Nothing came of that either. Five more people would die in that apartment before a man named Tracy Edwards escaped from it on the twenty-second of July and flagged down a squad car.

There is a version of this book that uses that story for its horror. This is not that book, and I am not going to spend the next several thousand words on what was found in the apartment, most of which is famous and none of which is necessary. What I want to do with Dahmer is narrower and, I think, more useful. I want to use him to explain something about comfort zones that the ordinary geographic version of the concept cannot explain by itself.

Because the thing that protected Jeffrey Dahmer on the night of May 27 was not a location. It was a set of assumptions carried by everyone who showed up.

The Anchor Point, Where It Was Ordinary

Start with what conforms, because a good deal of this case does.

Dahmer's first murder, in 1978, happened in Ohio, at his family's home, where he was living at the time. That is about as textbook an anchor point as the literature describes: the first killing occurs close to the residence, because the residence is where the offender is most comfortable and least conspicuous. Chapter 4 laid out the pattern. Dahmer's first crime follows it exactly.

Nine years passed before the next one. When the series resumed, it resumed in Milwaukee, where he had moved, first living with his grandmother in West Allis and later on his own at the Oxford Apartments. Both of those were anchor points in the conventional sense. He killed at his grandmother's house while he lived there. He killed in his apartment once he had one. The bodies stayed where he was, which is the single most common geographic fact about serial murder and the reason a residence search is so often the moment a case breaks open.

So at the level of where the killings happened, Dahmer is unremarkable. He killed at home, like most of them do.

The interesting part is not where he killed. It is where he hunted.

Where He Hunted Was Not a Neighborhood

Dahmer's hunting ground was a social world rather than a set of streets. Bars, bathhouses, a shopping mall, the places where a man could approach another man, start a conversation, make an offer, and leave with him without any of it looking like anything. He met his victims in a subculture, not in a district.

This is what I mean by an anchor point that is not a map. If you had run a geographic profile on the killings and looked only at where bodies and encounters were located, you would have gotten a workable but incomplete answer. The real zone was defined by the boundaries of a community: who was in it, what its norms were, and what kind of approach passed without comment inside it. Dahmer knew those norms. He had spent time in that world. He was, in the specific sense this book has been using the word, comfortable, and comfort is not a feeling here, it is an operational advantage. It means you know what will and will not draw attention.

The lecture version of this book has made the point for years in a single sentence, which I still think is the clearest way to say it. I would not move through a gay bar as easily as I would a straight one, because I do not know the unwritten rules of the room, only what I have seen on television. Someone who does know them can operate there. Someone who does not gets noticed, remembered, and described.

Substitute any bounded social world for the bar and the logic holds. A hospital ward. A church. A trucking route. A shelter. A group home. Anywhere a person can be a familiar and unremarkable presence, an offender who belongs there has the same advantage that a killer working his own neighborhood has, and for the same reason.

The pattern is not a Milwaukee anomaly. Five years before Dahmer's Milwaukee series resumed, and three years before it began, Dennis Nilsen was operating on the same principle in North London. Between December 1978 and January 1983, Nilsen killed at least twelve men at two addresses, first at 195 Melrose Avenue in Cricklewood and then at 23 Cranley Gardens in Muswell Hill, after meeting them at pubs and clubs in central London. He confessed to fifteen. He was a civil servant with a stable job and an ordinary flat, and he hunted in exactly the way Dahmer would - through a bounded social world, approaching men who were often homeless or drifting, whose disappearances would not immediately raise alarm. His first victim, Stephen Holmes, was fourteen years old. Nilsen was eventually caught in 1983 when human tissue clogged the drains at Cranley Gardens and a plumbing company was called out. Nothing about the linkage came from geographic analysis. It came from a blocked pipe. What the two cases share, across an ocean and half a decade, is not method or motive. It is the shape of the comfort zone: a subculture broad enough to move through, and a class of victim whose absence would go unremarked long enough for the pattern to compound.

Which means the practical instruction for an investigator is this: when the geography does not produce a pattern, do not conclude there is no comfort zone. Ask what the victims had in common besides where they were found. If the answer is a place they all passed through, an activity they all engaged in, or a world they all moved in, you have found the zone. It simply does not appear on a map.

The Pillar That Looks Broken and Is Not

Now the complication, and it is the reason Dahmer earns a chapter rather than a paragraph.

Chapter 4 established that offenders seldom cross racial and cultural barriers. Dahmer appears to blow a hole in that. He was a white man, and the majority of his victims were men of color, Black, Asian, and Hispanic. If the pattern were as simple as offenders killing people who look like them, Dahmer would be a straightforward refutation of it.

He is not, and understanding why sharpens the pillar considerably.

Go back to the mechanism rather than the correlation. The reason offenders tend to stay within their own group is not, in the main, a matter of preference. It is that an offender operates where he is unremarkable, and in most American cities, race and neighborhood are entangled tightly enough that staying unremarkable usually means staying within a racial group. The barrier is a byproduct of the comfort zone, not a separate rule.

Once you frame it that way, Dahmer stops being an exception. His comfort zone was a subculture, and that subculture was racially mixed. Within it, a white man approaching a Black man or an Asian man was not out of place, because the sorting principle in that room was not race. So the same mechanism that usually produces racial concordance produced racial discordance here, for exactly the same reason: he was operating where he did not stand out, and where he did not stand out happened to be a place where race did not mark him as an outsider.

That is the version of the pillar that survives contact with real cases. Offenders hunt where they blend. Most of the time that means their own racial group. Sometimes, when the comfort zone is defined by something other than geography, it does not. What never changes is the underlying requirement, which is that the offender must be able to move without attracting attention.

Chapter 4 put this as a caution about reading victim demographics too literally: a racially consistent victim set may only prove where the offender felt at home. Dahmer is the case that proves the point from the other side. A racially inconsistent victim set did not mean there was no comfort zone. It meant the zone was organized around something else.

The Part of the Zone Nobody Maps

Everything above concerns where an offender can move. There is a second dimension to the comfort zone, harder to see and, in this case, decisive, which concerns who gets believed.

Return to the street corner on May 27.

Three officers arrived to find a naked, injured, incoherent teenager and two young Black women telling them something was badly wrong. They also found a calm white man with a plausible explanation. They took the explanation. They did not check the boy's age. They did not take the witnesses' names. Glenda Cleveland spent the following days trying to get someone to revisit that decision, and could not, and later said that the boy had been let down as low as a person can be let down, which was to his grave.

Dahmer's neighbors said afterward what seems evident from the sequence: the witnesses were Black and the man was white, and so were the officers, and the account that got believed was the one that came from the person who looked least like a problem. I am not going to litigate the intent of three officers I have never met. Intent is not the point, and it is not what an investigator can work with. The point is what the outcome demonstrates about how these series persist.

Because there is a detail in this case that makes the failure not just a failure of judgment but a failure of records, and it is the one that ought to trouble anyone in this profession.

Two years earlier, in 1989, Dahmer had been convicted of second-degree sexual assault of a child. He served time at a work release camp and was on probation the night the officers walked Konerak Sinthasomphone back into that apartment. The child he had assaulted in the earlier case was Konerak's older brother.

The same family. Twice.

Nothing about that connection required a laboratory to find. It required someone to run a name and read a file. The information existed, in the possession of the criminal justice system, at the moment three officers were standing in the doorway deciding whether to believe him. What was missing was not evidence. It was the step that would have retrieved evidence already collected, and the reason that step was skipped is that nobody in that doorway thought the situation warranted it.

This is the linkage problem again, in a form that has nothing to do with forensics. Chapter 1 described the ordinary version: two files sitting in separate places, and no reason for anyone to put them side by side. Here the two files were closer together than that. They involved the same offender and the same household, and they still were not connected, because connecting them depended on a judgment about whether the situation was serious, and that judgment was made against the boy.

I can speak to how this works from the inside, at least as I saw it over twenty years in Los Angeles, and the honest version is less about malice than about structure and attention. Street-level calls and missing persons reports get triaged, and the triage runs on things that have nothing to do with how dangerous the underlying situation actually is. Whether a case is likely to draw outside attention. Whether a family has the persistence, and the standing, to keep the case in front of someone who can act on it. Those are uncomfortable things to write down, but any honest detective will tell you they are real, and in the largest departments they are closer to the rule than the exception. At the top, a big-city department is a political institution, and it answers to pressures applied from above, which means the cases that generate pressure get worked and the cases that generate none can drift.

The exception, and it is a crucial one, is the individual detective who keeps working a case that is not officially in front of him, or that sits low in the triage, because he sees something the system does not: a pattern, a targeted neighborhood, a victim type that keeps recurring. Those detectives exist and they are the reason a number of these series were ever connected at all. I knew some of them. Mitzi Roberts, who worked Robbery-Homicide and later cold cases, was one of the good ones, the kind who would keep pulling a file because she could not let go of it, and who treated the forensic side of the house as partners in the work rather than as technicians to be ordered around. That mattered more than she probably knew. The detective makes the call on what gets worked and what a forensic unit even responds to. On the forensic end we had zero control over any of that. We worked the cases we were assigned, and only those. No case book of our own, no independent files, no ability to notice across cases that two scenes we had photographed years apart might belong together. If the connection was going to be made, a detective was going to have to make it.

I want to say something about what that costs, because the trope of the dedicated detective usually stops at the point where the case gets solved, and the truth runs past it. I worked with another detective at Robbery-Homicide, one of the finest I ever knew, who valued his privacy enough that I will not name him here. He traveled the world, literally, to close cases, following killers across borders most people never think a homicide detective crosses. He was generous in the small ways that hold a working relationship together; he used to bring me back local liquor from places I would never get to, things you could not buy in the States. And he carried a caseload that would have flattened most people. It flattened him, eventually. After several days of migraines and a workload that would kill an ox, he walked into his own house and had a massive stroke, more or less the moment he got home. The system does not have a line item for that. The detectives who keep pulling files nobody assigned them, who see the pattern the structure is built to miss, are running on something the structure does not replenish, and some of them run all the way out. When I say the connection depends on an individual rather than a system, I do not mean it as an inspirational point. I mean that we are asking specific, named, mortal people to compensate for a gap in the machinery, and it takes a real toll on the ones who actually do it. He kept working for several years afterwards, after he was forced to retire. He would get called back in to finish cases that he worked, and to brief Detectives that were going to testify on his cases. He could not testify in Court, for obvious reasons, but after 3 years, he was able to requalify with is pistol. A milestone for a man who dedicated his life to his work, and was no longer able to do it the way he felt he should.

He kept working for several years after the stroke forced him to retire. They would call him back in to close out cases he had worked, and to brief the detectives who were going to testify on them. He could not take the stand himself anymore, for obvious reasons, but he could still hand the work off properly, which for a man like him was not nothing. After three years he requalified with his pistol. That is the kind of milestone that means little to anyone who did not do the job and everything to a man who had given it his life and could no longer do it the way he believed it should be done

There is a structural reason the connections get missed, and it is worth laying out plainly, because it is the geographic version of the linkage problem from Chapter 1. When I left, Los Angeles was divided into twenty-one geographic patrol Divisions, grouped under four geographic Bureaus, Central, West, Valley, and South, policing roughly four million people across four hundred and sixty-eight square miles. A geographic Division sees what happens inside its own boundaries. It is very good at spotting a pattern within those boundaries and structurally blind to one that crosses them. A killer who takes one victim in one Division and the next victim two Divisions over has, without intending to, defeated the unit of analysis, because no single Division is looking at both.

This is why the specialized, non-geographic Divisions matter so much, and why the trope that the system simply ignores certain victims is both true and incomplete. At the local geographic level, some cases genuinely do get less attention, and cases involving sex workers are the standard example. But the overarching Divisions, Robbery-Homicide chief among them, along with the Bureau-level homicide units, look at exactly those cases specifically for patterns, precisely because they sit high enough to see across the boundaries a series exploits. Robbery-Homicide oversees work that spans the Bureaus; the Bureaus sit above the Divisions. The higher the desk a file lands on, the more of the city it can see at once, and whether a series becomes visible depends less on anyone's competence than on how high up the pattern finally reaches someone with the altitude to recognize it. When that recognition happened at Robbery-Homicide in my era, it was often independent, a particular detective connecting the dots, rather than a systematic function that guaranteed the dots would be connected at all.

Victim Selection, Read Honestly

Chapter 2 introduced the framework the FBI Symposium uses for victim selection: availability, vulnerability, and desirability. Dahmer is a clear illustration of all three, and reading him through that lens says something uncomfortable about how these cases get worked.

Availability was the subculture. He met people where he could meet them.

Desirability was his own preference pattern, which is the part that belongs to the psychologists and which I will leave to them.

Vulnerability is the one that matters here, because vulnerability in the Symposium's sense is not only about physical capacity to resist. It is about exposure: how likely is an attack on this person to be interrupted, reported, believed, and investigated. And by that definition, Dahmer selected for vulnerability with considerable precision, whether or not he could have articulated it that way. Young men. Men of color. Men whose families were immigrants, or poor, or both. Men whose absence would be reported to a system that has, historically and measurably, worked those reports differently than it works others.

I want to be careful here, because there is a lazy version of this argument that I am not making. I am not saying the offender sat down and calculated the response rate of the Milwaukee Police Department by victim demographic. I am saying something simpler and better supported by how these series actually run. An offender does not need to understand the system to benefit from it. He only needs to keep doing what has worked so far. Dahmer killed, and nothing happened, and so he killed again. The absence of consequence is the feedback, and the feedback shaped the pattern regardless of whether he ever reasoned about why the consequences did not come.

That is the honest methodological statement, and it has a practical edge to it. If an offender's victim pool is drawn from a population whose disappearances get less investigative attention, then the offender's effective comfort zone includes that gap in attention. It is as real a part of his operating environment as the streets he knows. And unlike his geography, it is something the profession can actually change.

The Photographs

One more element of the Dahmer case is worth isolating, because it connects him to a case at the opposite end of the country, and the connection says something about trophies that neither case says alone.

Dahmer took Polaroids. He photographed his victims, and the photographs were in the apartment when it was finally searched. They were part of what made the scale of the case immediately apparent to the officers who walked in, and part of what tied him to victims who might otherwise have taken far longer to identify.

Now hold that image next to the one this book opened with, because I want to place the two deliberately side by side. The prologue described a different search, in a different decade, two and a half thousand miles away: the garage of a house in South Los Angeles, a false wall, and behind it nearly a thousand photographs and hundreds of hours of video. That was the Grim Sleeper, Lonnie Franklin Jr., a case I worked and one I will come to in full later in this book. For now, set Franklin's hidden compartment beside Dahmer's apartment and notice what the two have in common, because it is almost the only thing they have in common.

Jeffrey Dahmer and Franklin were about as different as two serial killers can be. Different cities, different decades, different victim pools, different methods, different everything. Dahmer killed men in Milwaukee and kept them in his apartment. Franklin killed women in Los Angeles across a span of twenty-five years. They never crossed paths, shared nothing, and belong to entirely separate chapters of this book. And each of them, independently, photographed his victims and could not throw the photographs away.

That is the point of setting them together. When the same specific behavior turns up in two offenders who have nothing else in common, the behavior is telling you something structural rather than personal. The trophy is not a souvenir of an event; it is the continuation of the event, which is why it gets kept rather than discarded, and why a man will hide it behind a wall for twenty-five years rather than destroy the single most incriminating thing he owns. Chapter 4 argued that a trophy is the most direct physical link available between an offender and a scene he has otherwise cleaned. Dahmer and Franklin are that argument, made twice, independently, twenty-five hundred miles and a dozen years apart. In both cases the photographs are part of what turned a suspect into a defendant.

There is a specific reason photographs, of all the objects an offender might keep, sit at the center of this argument.

Most trophies are objects an offender takes from a victim: clothing, jewelry, an item from a wallet, a personal effect the victim would have carried. Those objects tie the offender to a scene, but each one ties him to one scene, and the connection has to be established forensically once the object is recovered. A photograph does something structurally different. A photograph is generative. It creates a record the offender did not have before, of a specific victim, at a specific moment, in a form that can be reviewed and revisited by the offender himself. It is the only category of trophy that increases in number over the course of a series without any object being taken. It is also the only category that, once recovered, can independently establish the identity of victims the investigation may not yet have connected to the offender at all.

This is why Dahmer's Polaroids and the archive behind the wall of a garage in South Los Angeles were both, in different decades and with different technology, the pieces of evidence that established scale. Neither one produced a single link at a time. Each one produced an inventory. And the inventory, once catalogued, closed cases that had been open for years.

A ring or a scarf recovered from an offender's home is evidence. A hundred photographs, or a wall of catalogued videotape, is a solved series.

A word on the rest of it, since it will occur to every reader and I would rather address it plainly than pretend it is not there. The post-mortem conduct in the Dahmer case is the most famous thing about him and the reason his name is a shorthand. Chapter 3 gave the numbers on those behaviors, and they are rare, in the low single digits of cases, and they are dramatically overrepresented in fiction precisely because they are rare.

Dahmer is famous because Dahmer is unusual. Building a general model of serial murder out of him is like forming a picture of commercial aviation from crash footage, and I said as much in the myths chapter. The reason he is in this book is not his notoriety. It is the comfort zone.

What This Case Actually Teaches

Seventeen victims, from 1978 to 1991. A conviction in 1992 on fifteen counts in Wisconsin, with more admitted. Thirteen years, one offender, and a series that was interrupted twice by the criminal justice system, once by a conviction and once by three officers standing in a doorway, and continued both times.

The lesson people take from Dahmer is usually about the man. The lesson available from Dahmer is about the environment he operated in.

His comfort zone had three layers. The geographic one was ordinary and would have been visible to any competent analysis: he killed where he lived. The social one was the hunting ground, a subculture rather than a district, which is the layer that geographic profiling alone would have missed and the reason this chapter exists. And the third layer was not a place at all. It was the reliable, repeated fact that when his account was set against his victims' accounts, his was the one that got accepted.

An offender does not choose that third layer. He inherits it. But it functions exactly like the other two, and it is worth naming as part of the same pattern, because it is the only one of the three that the profession has any power to alter. We cannot make offenders stop hunting where they are comfortable. We can decide, as a matter of practice, whose call gets taken seriously at two in the morning, and whose name gets written down.

Konerak Sinthasomphone's did not.

ON THE RECORD

Established

- **A comfort zone can be social rather than geographic.** Dahmer killed at his residences, which is ordinary, but hunted inside a subculture, which a map-based analysis would not have shown.

- **The racial-barrier pattern is a byproduct, not a rule.** Offenders stay where they are unremarkable. Usually that means their own group. Dahmer's zone was a racially mixed subculture, so the same mechanism produced the opposite result.
- **Vulnerability includes whether a victim will be believed.** The Symposium framework treats vulnerability as exposure to attack without interruption or response. That includes the response of the system.
- **Trophies behave the same way across unrelated cases.** Dahmer kept photographs. So did the Grim Sleeper. In both cases the kept images were central to establishing the scale of the series.

Myth

- **That Dahmer disproves the comfort zone.** He is one of the clearest demonstrations of it, once the zone is understood as social rather than cartographic.
- **That the famous post-mortem behavior is typical.** It appears in a very small percentage of cases and is heavily overrepresented in fiction. It is why he is famous, not why he is instructive.

What the record shows

- **The information needed was already in the system.** Dahmer was on probation for assaulting a child from the same family at the moment officers accepted his account. Retrieving that required a name check, not a laboratory.
- **Five more people died after the first call.** The failure was not a single decision but a sustained refusal to revisit it despite repeated attempts by a neighbor to force the issue.

Chapter 8: What the Data Misses, Women Who Kill

The reservoir was the giveaway, though it took me a while to understand why.

The case involved a woman who found wealthy older men, made herself part of their lives, and then, once she was inside, had them robbed of everything and disposed of in a Los Angeles reservoir. I described it briefly a few chapters ago, in the context of the myth that serial killers are all men, and I want to return to it here at greater length, because it is the clearest example I personally worked of the thing this chapter is about. Women who kill serially do exist, they are consistently underestimated as suspects, and the reason they are underestimated is the same reason they are hard to catch: they do not look like what everyone is looking for.

This chapter is titled what it is because the standard data on serial murder, accurate as far as it goes, systematically undercounts and misreads female offenders. Not through any conspiracy, and not through bad statistics. Through the same mechanism that runs through this entire book. We find what we look for, we look for what we expect, and almost nobody expects a woman.

But I want to correct an impression I may have given in earlier chapters, because getting this right matters to the whole argument of the book. It would be easy to conclude that female serial killers somehow break the four pillars, that they operate outside the framework this book has spent six chapters building. They do not. The pillars hold for them exactly as they hold for anyone else. What changes is that the pillars are harder to see, because the dominant female motive, financial gain, disguises each one. The comfort zone looks like hospitality. The signature looks like natural death. The trophy looks like bookkeeping. The methodology is not failing on these offenders. It is being camouflaged by them, and the camouflage is the thing worth understanding.

The Number, and Why It Is Probably Low

Chapter 3 gave the figure: women are roughly nine to eleven percent of known serial killers, and that share has been falling for a century, from about a third before 1930 to around six percent since 1980. I stand by those numbers as the best available, and I also think they are an undercount, for a reason that follows directly from how women tend to kill.

The methods historically associated with female offenders are quiet ones. Poison. Smothering. The gradual medical decline of someone already old or sick or dependent. A man strangled in an alley generates a homicide investigation. An elderly boarder who simply stops waking up generates a death certificate. The first is a case. The second is a Tuesday. And a killing that is never recorded as a killing never enters the database that tells us how many female serial killers there are.

So when the data says women are a small and shrinking share of serial killers, it is telling the truth about the cases we caught. It is not necessarily telling the truth about the cases that happened. The decline since 1930 is real, and Chapter 2 gave the likely reason, modern toxicology and recordkeeping closing off the poisoning methods that once worked. But the same closing-off that reduced the number also improved our ability to detect what remained, which means the historical figures are almost certainly an undercount of a kind we can no longer measure. We are better at catching them now precisely because we were so bad at it before.

That undercount argument is not a hunch. It shows up in the method data as soon as you sort it by sex. The Radford and Florida Gulf Coast University Serial Killer Database's 2023 annual report cross-tabulates offender sex against method for every case in its files, and the disparity in one column is extraordinary. Two hundred and seventeen women in the database used poison, which is 54.5 percent of the female-offender sample. Ninety-eight men used poison, which is 2.4 percent of the male-offender sample. A factor of more than twenty. On a sample of roughly four thousand offenders total, that is not statistical noise. It is the single largest method disparity in the sex-difference data, and it means the female serial killers we do count concentrate heavily in the one method most likely to be missed on first pass by a coroner's office.

One caution that belongs alongside those numbers, because Chapter 3 and Chapter 5 both leaned on the IQ-by-method figures. The IQ cell for poisoners in the Radford database rests on a single person. The overall female-offender IQ sample runs to twelve, against three hundred and eleven men. Any argument about whether female poisoners score differently from male poisoners cannot be made from that data; the intersection cell is too small to say anything about. What the sex-difference data does support, robustly, is the method choice itself. The women who become identifiable serial killers use poison at more than twenty times the male rate, and that finding does not depend on the IQ column at all.

Money, Not Blood

The single most consistent finding about female serial killers is motive, and it separates them cleanly from the male pattern.

Men who kill serially do so, disproportionately, for reasons rooted in the act itself, power, control, thrill, the enjoyment categories from Chapter 3. Women who kill serially do so, disproportionately, for money. The killing is a means. It is instrumental in a way that a great deal of male serial murder is not, and that difference shapes everything about how these cases look, why they persist, and how they are eventually broken.

The victim data reinforces the point in a way that is harder to argue with than the motive interviews are. Radford's 2023 report separates victim characteristics by offender sex, and the differences do not read as gradations of the same pattern. They read as different patterns entirely. Fourteen percent of female serial killer primary victims are infants, against less than half a percent of male offenders'. Nearly eight percent are children between two and twelve, against three percent for male offenders. Male offenders' victims are almost never family members; female offenders' victims are, more often than not, family members - spouses, stepchildren, elderly parents, patients in their care. Male offenders overwhelmingly select victims of one sex, most often female; female offenders overwhelmingly select victims of both sexes, because they are not hunting a demographic. They are killing whoever comes into their sphere.

Set the two victim profiles side by side and the reason the female cases are systematically undercounted becomes structural rather than mysterious. An infant death enters the medical system before it enters the criminal one. A frail elderly patient's decline enters a doctor's office before it enters a homicide detective's caseload. A husband dying of what looks like a heart attack becomes a life-insurance question before it becomes an investigative one. The homicide-detection apparatus this book has spent seven chapters describing was built to catch the offender who leaves a body. It was not built to catch the offender who signs a death certificate.

An instrumental killer behaves differently from an expressive one, and this is where the pillars start to wear their disguise. She still has a comfort zone, but because she is not hunting, it does not look like a hunting ground; her victims come to her, or are already in her care, so the zone reads as a home or a workplace rather than a stalking territory. She still has a signature, but because the ritual is a repeated practical method rather than an expressive flourish, it reads as routine rather than compulsion. She still keeps a trophy, but the trophy is the money, or what the money buys, which reads as motive rather than souvenir. Every pillar is present. Each one is dressed as something ordinary.

One other quantitative finding is worth naming here because it fits the same pattern. Radford's data shows female serial killers are, on average, about four years older than male serial killers at the start of their series - 31.6 versus 27.8. That is a real difference on a sample that size, and it does not reflect maturity or restraint. It reflects the fact that instrumental crimes require positioning. You cannot become the sole caregiver to a wealthy elderly boarder in your twenties. You cannot marry three men and outlive them by thirty. The setup takes time, and the age-at-onset data records that setup. The male offender who kills for expressive reasons can begin as soon as the compulsion catches up to him. The female offender who kills for instrumental ones has to build the environment first.

This is why she is hard to catch, and it has nothing to do with cleverness. The methodology of detection leans heavily on reading the non-functional parts of a crime, the ritual, the trophy, the thing done for its own sake, because those parts point directly at the offender. When the offender is instrumental, those same elements are still there but they are functional, folded into a scheme that looks like ordinary life. The signature is real, but it hides inside a plausible medical decline. The trophy is real, but it hides inside a bank account. You are not looking at an absence of evidence. You are looking at evidence wearing a disguise, and the disguise is made of normalcy.

The Structural Parallel

Chapter 5 planted a comparison that belongs here, and it is worth cashing in explicitly. Ted Kaczynski's bombs and Nannie Doss's stewed prunes are, mechanically, the same move. Both are methods that keep the offender absent at the moment of death. Both require preparation before the fact and produce no confrontation during it. Both leave scenes that are hard to read, because the offender was somewhere else when the reading materials were made.

The population that selects each method is different, and it is different for reasons this chapter has been describing. A bomb requires technical capability that concentrates in a small population, disproportionately male, historically well-educated, and rare enough in the record that Radford's bomber IQ figure rests on three people. A poison requires access - to a substance, and to a victim whose ordinary decline will not immediately raise alarm - that concentrates in a different small population, disproportionately female, working in caregiving or family roles, and common enough in the record that Radford's female-poisoner sample is over two hundred cases.

What the two methods share, structurally, is not who selects them but what selection accomplishes. Absence at the moment of death is worth the effort of preparation because presence at the moment of death is the single thing most likely to produce the evidence the four pillars work from. Kaczynski and the female poisoner are, in this narrow behavioral sense, using the same discipline against the same detection apparatus. They are choosing methods that make the crime harder to see.

That parallel does not make them the same offender. Kaczynski was expressive, driven by an ideology he needed the world to hear; the classic female poisoner is instrumental, killing for what she gets. What the parallel shows is that method choice is a separate axis from motive, and that a chapter organized around either alone will miss offenders who share one but not the other. It also shows that the discipline the female offenders demonstrate - patience, preparation, absence - is not incompatible with the male offenders the book has already described. It is a technique that some offenders in both groups converge on, for the same operational reason. It gets them out of the room before the evidence is made.

Dorothea Puente

The clearest American example is Dorothea Puente, and her case is worth telling with some care, because almost every element of it illustrates the pattern.

Through the 1980s, Puente ran a boarding house in Sacramento that took in exactly the people a city has the least apparatus for missing: the elderly, the disabled, the addicted, the mentally ill, the poor. She presented as a kindly grandmother, cooked for her tenants, set up their Social Security accounts, and by outward appearance provided a genuine service to people society had few other places for. What she was actually doing was drugging them, burying them in the yard, and continuing to cash their benefit checks. Seven bodies were eventually recovered from the property. She was charged with nine murders and convicted of three, the jury deadlocking on the rest, in part, jurors later suggested, because they could not reconcile the grandmother in front of them with the crimes described.

Read Puente against the four pillars and, at first glance, she seems to have none of them. Look again and she has all four; they are simply hiding in plain sight. Her comfort zone was as real as any hunter's, tighter than most, in fact: her own home, so familiar and controlled that the victims came to her and died where she lived. Her signature was real, a specific and repeated pharmacological mèthod, the same drugs, the same burial, the same story told to anyone who asked, which is exactly the recurring, offender-specific ritual that Chapter 4 defined; a forensic examiner who noticed identical drug profiles across multiple bodies would be reading Puente's signature directly. Her trophy was real, too. It was the Social Security checks she kept cashing after the tenants who earned them were in the yard, because for the offender who kills for gain, the money and what it provides is precisely the thing kept and returned to, which is what a trophy is. Only the racial-and-cultural pillar is quiet in her case, and it is quiet not because she violates it but because it went untested; her victims were her own local, largely same-group tenants, so no barrier was ever crossed. Four pillars, all present, none of them announcing themselves, and she killed nine people in plain view of a whole neighborhood.

That is the real lesson of Dorothea Puente, and it is the opposite of the one it looks like. She does not show that the methodology fails on female offenders. She shows that the methodology has to be read through the motive. Change the motive from expression to money, and every pillar keeps operating while changing its outward appearance. The hunting ground becomes a boarding house. The ritual becomes a caregiving routine. The trophy becomes an income stream. An investigator who expects the pillars to look the way they look in a male sexual-homicide case will glance at Puente and see nothing, which is exactly what a jury did when it deadlocked on six of her nine counts, unable to square the grandmother with the graves.

And notice what finally broke the case. Not forensics. Not a pattern recognized by an analyst. A social worker named Judy Moise reported one tenant, Alvaro Montoya, missing, and pushed, and would not let it go. The investigation began because one person with a professional obligation to a vulnerable man refused to accept that he had simply wandered off. That is the same thread that ran through the last chapter. These victims were, in the phrase the coverage of the case used, shadow people, and shadow people generate no urgency on their own. Someone has to generate it for them.

The Longer Lineage

Puente is not an anomaly, and she is not modern. Female serial killers are among the oldest documented offenders on record, which is worth stating plainly because the culture keeps forgetting it. Chapter 3 noted that the film Monster marketed Aileen Wuornos as America's first female serial killer, and that the claim is not merely wrong but wrong by centuries. Here is the lineage that claim erases.

Jane Toppan is worth pausing on, because she is both a vivid case and a useful exception. Born Honora Kelley in Boston to Irish immigrants around the middle of the 1800s, orphaned young, she trained as a nurse and turned the profession into an instrument. That is the first thing to mark about her, and it recurs across this whole category: the caregiving professions place a person in intimate, trusted, unsupervised contact with the sick, the old, and the dependent, and a small number of people have always understood that access as opportunity. A nurse who kills does not need a comfort zone in the geographic sense. The ward is the comfort zone. The bedside is the anchor point. She belongs there, she is expected there, and no one questions why she is alone with a patient who then declines.

Toppan's method was morphine and atropine, and here the signature pillar is unusually literal. She did not simply poison; she adjusted doses to bring patients to the edge of death and back again, more than once, before finally letting them die. That is not an efficient way to kill for gain. It is a ritual, in precisely the sense Chapter 4 meant, behavior that serves the offender rather than the crime, and Toppan's ritual served something she herself described in disturbing terms after her arrest. She admitted a compulsion to it, an appetite, and told her examiners she aspired to have killed more helpless people than anyone who had ever lived. She confessed to thirty-one killings and was suspected of many more. She is, in other words, one of the clearest exceptions to the money-motive rule this chapter has been building: an expressive female serial killer, driven by the act itself rather than by gain, which is rare enough among women that it made her a national sensation and confounds the tidy version of the pattern. I include her precisely because she does not fit. The pattern is a strong tendency, not a law, and Toppan is the reminder that a real category always has real exceptions inside it.

Mary Ann Cotton, working in England across the middle decades of the 1800s, is the counterweight to Toppan and the purer example of the dominant pattern. She moved through husbands, children, and stepchildren by poison over many years, collecting insurance money as she went, a black-widow scheme sustained across a body count that likely reached into the high teens or beyond. Where Toppan killed for the experience, Cotton killed for the payout, and she is the older, quieter template that Puente would echo a century later on another continent.

Nannie Doss, whom the American press of the 1950s gleefully named the Giggling Granny for her demeanor under questioning, is the case that shows how even the money motive is not always clean. Across roughly three decades ending with her arrest in 1954, Doss poisoned a series of family members, including four of her five husbands, with arsenic, which she folded into stewed prunes, coffee, and moonshine. She was convicted of one murder, her fifth husband's, and confessed to several more; investigators suspected as many as eleven victims. She did take out insurance policies, and part of her motive was plainly financial. But by her own account something stranger drove her too: a lifelong diet of romance magazines had left her searching, husband after husband, for an idealized love none of them provided, and she killed the ones who fell short. Doss sits deliberately at the seam of this chapter's argument. Her comfort zone was domestic, her signature was arsenic in a sweet vehicle, her trophies were insurance payouts, and yet her motive was not purely instrumental at all. She is the case that keeps the money-motive pattern honest by showing its edges.

Set those names in a row and two things stand out. The first is the timespan: from the 1800s to the 1950s to the 1980s, an unbroken line, which by itself refutes the idea that the female serial killer is a recent or exotic figure. The second is the method. Poison, poison, poison, medical routine. These are the quiet killings, the ones that leave a body that does not look like a crime scene, and they are quiet not by accident but because quiet is what let them continue. The loud ones were caught. The quiet ones wrote their own body counts.

The pattern is not confined to the historical record. Beverley Allitt, a British nurse, murdered four children on a hospital children's ward and attempted to murder three more, causing grievous bodily harm to six others, over the course of a fifty-nine-day period in 1991 before the pattern was recognized. Her method was insulin and potassium injections. Her comfort zone was a specific ward, in a specific hospital, on shifts she was rostered to. Her victim pool was patients whose fragile conditions would explain, at first glance, any sudden deterioration. She was convicted in 1993 and received thirteen life sentences, and the psychiatric finding at trial was Munchausen syndrome by proxy, a compulsion to produce medical crises in others in order to be seen managing them. That motive is worth marking, because it is neither the money of the classic poisoner nor the expressive drive of the male sexual offender. It is a third thing, and it sits at the same seam Nannie Doss occupied: a case that keeps the money-motive pattern honest by showing its edges.

Set her case against the Charles Cullen material from Chapter 4 and the pattern surfaces clearly. Cullen, a male nurse in Pennsylvania and New Jersey, moved across ten institutions over sixteen years, killing patients whose deaths did not initially register as suspicious. He was caught by cross-institutional records that finally added up. His British counterpart in this section was caught within two months of her first murder, by a consultant who saw the pattern of cardiac arrests on the ward and did not accept it as coincidence. Both offenders used the anchor-as-role logic Chapter 4 described. Both selected victims whose absence would not immediately raise alarm, in Cullen's case by moving between institutions, in Allitt's by working a ward where clinical decline was expected. The methodology reaches both cases. The pillars translate, and the specific institutional and demographic contexts change what each pillar looks like in operation, but the logic underneath does not change at all.

The pattern lives in modern medicine because modern medicine still contains what the pattern requires: professional access to the vulnerable, a plausible explanation for sudden death, and institutional structures that do not, by default, look across their own boundaries at a run of quiet decompensations. Toppan a century ago and this nurse in the 1990s were doing structurally similar work in structurally similar environments, which is why they were both caught late.

Aileen Wuornos, and Why She Was the Exception

Which brings us to Wuornos herself, the woman the culture mistook for the beginning of the story when she was closer to an aberration within it.

Between 1989 and 1990, Aileen Wuornos shot and robbed seven men in Florida, men who had picked her up while she was working as a prostitute along the highways. She was executed in 2002. Her case became the subject of the film that fixed her, wrongly, as the archetypal female serial killer in the public mind.

The irony is that Wuornos was atypical of female serial killers in nearly every respect. She used a firearm, where the female pattern is poison and smothering. She killed strangers, where the female pattern is intimates and dependents. Her killings were violent and immediate, where the female pattern is gradual and medical. She was, if anything, killing in a recognizably male pattern, which is very likely part of why she became famous: she was legible. She did the thing everyone already understood a serial killer to do, and so she could be seen. The Puentes and the Toppans and the Dosses, killing quietly across decades, were far more representative and far less visible, and the visibility is the whole problem.

This is the trap the data sets, restated in human terms. Wuornos is overrepresented in the culture because she fit the template. The women who did not fit the template are underrepresented in the data for the identical reason. What is easy to see gets recorded, studied, filmed, and remembered. What is hard to see gets a death certificate and a quiet burial, and never becomes a case at all.

The Reservoir, in Full

I want to come back to my own case now, because it sits at an interesting angle to everything above: a female offender who was neither purely instrumental nor purely expressive, and who was caught not by reading a signature but by physics.

What I can say, standing back from the specifics, is what the case taught me and why it belongs at the center of this chapter rather than as a footnote to it. The offender did not fit the template, and the not-fitting was not incidental to how long she operated. Investigators look for a certain shape, and she was not that shape, and the gap between what she was and what anyone was looking for was, functionally, her comfort zone. She hid inside a category assumption. Chapter 6 argued that a comfort zone can be a subculture rather than a place. This case argues that it can also be a blind spot, the space created by everyone's shared and incorrect certainty about who does this kind of thing.

And she was caught, in the end, by the most ordinary forensic work imaginable. Not a psychological insight, not a profile, not a leap. A shoe print, badly photographed by someone who did not know what he had, reconstructed by measuring the things in the frame whose sizes could be known and working back to the thing that could not. That is the whole book in one image. The methodology does not care what shape the offender is. It measures what is there.

What This Chapter Actually Argues

It would be easy to read all of this as a claim that female serial killers are secretly common, or secretly more dangerous, and that is not the argument. The argument is narrower and, I think, more useful.

The tools this book has described are very good at catching a particular kind of offender: the one who hunts, who ritualizes, who keeps, who expresses. That offender is disproportionately male, and the methodology was, to a significant degree, built by studying him. The offender who kills instrumentally, quietly, for gain, from within a position of trust, is disproportionately female, and she is partially invisible to those same tools, not because she is smarter but because the tools were calibrated on someone else.

That is not a reason to distrust the methodology. It is a reason to know its edges. Every method has a population it was built on and a population it misses, and the honest practitioner keeps both in view. The woman in the boarding house and the woman at the reservoir were not caught by the standard playbook. They were caught, when they were caught at all, by someone who noticed that the standard playbook was returning a negative on a situation that nonetheless felt wrong, and kept pulling the thread anyway.

The data misses them. Good investigators, occasionally, do not. The difference between those two sentences is the entire reason this chapter exists.

ON THE RECORD

Established

- **Women are a real but small share of known serial killers.** Roughly nine to eleven percent, declining since 1930, and the recorded figure is probably an undercount because the classic female methods often escaped detection entirely.
- **The dominant female motive is financial gain.** Where male serial murder skews expressive, female serial murder skews instrumental. The killing is a means, not the point.
- **The four pillars hold for female killers; they just hide.** The money motive disguises each one. The comfort zone looks like a home, the signature like a caregiving routine, the trophy like a bank balance. The methodology is camouflaged, not defeated.
- **The caregiving professions recur.** Toppan and Puente both used positions of trust and access to the vulnerable. Proximity plus authority plus low scrutiny is a repeating structure.

Myth

- **That Aileen Wuornos was the first, or the archetype.** She was neither. Female serial killers predate the nation, and Wuornos was atypical precisely because she killed in a recognizably male pattern, which is part of why she became visible.

— **That the low female percentage is the whole story.** It reflects the cases caught, not necessarily the cases committed. Quiet methods produce death certificates, not homicide files.

What the record shows

— **Puente killed nine, was convicted of three.** The gap was not evidentiary weakness so much as a jury unable to reconcile the grandmother with the crimes, which is the misread this chapter is about, sitting in a verdict.

— **Both signature cases here broke on a person, not a pattern.** Puente on a social worker who would not drop it; the reservoir case on ordinary forensic reconstruction. Neither fit the profile, and neither was caught by the profile.

Chapter 9: Samuel Little and the Undercount Problem

For most of his life, the most prolific serial killer in American history was right, and we were wrong.

Samuel Little believed he would never be caught. Not because he was brilliant, and not because he was careful in the way the fictional masterminds are careful. He believed it for a colder and more accurate reason, which a ViCAP crime analyst put as plainly as it can be put after the case finally broke: Little thought no one was accounting for his victims. He was very nearly correct. He strangled women for thirty-five years, from 1970 to 2005, and for almost all of that time the system that was supposed to be counting simply was not.

This chapter is the one the whole book has been building toward, because Samuel Little is not just another case study. He is the undercount problem made flesh, the single largest demonstration in the American record of everything that goes wrong when the linkage that this book is about does not happen. Every failure described in the preceding chapters, the geographic blindness, the victims who generate no urgency, the deaths that never get recorded as crimes, the series that stays invisible because nobody assembles it, all of it converges in one man who killed more people than Bundy and Gacy combined and was, for decades, functionally invisible while doing it.

The Numbers, and What They Mean

Let me state the figures carefully, because they are the spine of the chapter and they are frequently mangled.

Little confessed to 93 murders. The FBI's Violent Criminal Apprehension Program has independently confirmed at least 50 of them, a number that has continued to climb as cases are matched, and FBI analysts have stated they consider all 93 confessions credible. He is, by the confirmed count alone, the most prolific serial killer in United States history, ahead of every name the public actually knows. He killed, by his own account, between

1970 and 2005, nearly all of his victims women, many of them strangled and then left in ways that did not read, at the time, as homicide.

Hold those two numbers next to each other: 93 confessed, and for decades, close to zero attributed. That gap is not like the Grim Sleeper gap between DNA linkage and courtroom conviction, where the evidence existed and the prosecution was strategic. This gap is worse, because for most of those thirty-five years the murders were not sitting in a file waiting to be linked. Many of them were not classified as murders at all.

This is the part that matters most, and I want to be exact about it. According to the FBI, many of Little's victims' deaths were originally ruled overdoses, or attributed to accidental or undetermined causes. Some of the bodies were never found. Think about what that means for the linkage problem this book has been describing. Chapter 1 imagined two homicide files that no one thought to put side by side. Little's case is worse than that. In many instances there was no homicide file to misplace, because the death had been written down as something other than a killing. You cannot link cases that were never recorded as cases.

Why He Was Invisible

Everything this book has taught applies to Samuel Little, and it applies in the direction of explaining his invisibility rather than his capture. Run him through the pillars and the framework and you do not get a profile of a criminal genius. You get a profile of the perfect blind spot.

Start with victim selection, because it is the whole engine of the case. Little preyed, overwhelmingly, on women who were poor, who were addicted, who were involved in prostitution, who were Black, who were transient, who were in some combination of all of these. In the language of the FBI Symposium framework from Chapter 2, he selected for vulnerability with lethal precision, and vulnerability, remember, is not primarily about physical capacity to resist. It is about exposure: how likely an attack is to be interrupted, reported, believed, and investigated. Little's victims scored at the very bottom of that scale on every axis. They were women whose disappearances often went unreported, whose deaths were often uninvestigated, and whose bodies, when found, were often filed under overdose or misadventure and forgotten.

This connects directly to the argument of the last two chapters, and it is worth making the connection explicit. Chapter 6 described how Jeffrey Dahmer's victims were drawn from populations whose reports the system worked differently. Chapter 7 described how Dorothea Puente's victims were shadow people whose disappearances generated no urgency on their own. Samuel Little is those same observations at national scale, sustained for thirty-five years. He did not need a comfort zone in the geographic sense, and in fact he was mobile, killing across many states, which ordinarily makes an offender easier to spot, not harder. He got away with mobility precisely because his victim selection made each individual killing disappear into the background noise of a system that was not accounting for those particular deaths. His comfort zone was not a place. It was a category of victim the system had decided, in practice if never in policy, not to count.

That is the uncomfortable center of this case, and I am going to state it as a methodological fact rather than a moral one, because the methodology is my lane and the fact stands on its own. An offender who selects victims the system does not prioritize inherits, for free, the single most valuable asset a serial killer can have: time. Time to develop, time to repeat, time to refine, and above all time before anyone assembles the pattern. Little had thirty-five years of it. He did not steal that time through cleverness. It was handed to him by a set of choices, made across countless individual cases by countless individual people, about which victims warranted the full weight of an investigation and which did not.

The Mobility Inversion

Mobility is the other half of the answer, and reading it against Chapter 6 makes the point sharper than either chapter can make alone.

Little's rap sheet, when it was finally assembled, spanned twenty-four states over fifty-six years and contained nearly a hundred arrests. He served less than ten years in prison across all of it. His victims, once the confessions and confirmations came in, spanned at least nineteen states between 1970 and 2005. He was, by any measure the standard literature uses, an extraordinarily mobile offender.

Chapter 6 argued that mobility usually exposes an offender rather than protecting him. Ted Bundy is the case in point: a stranger in every environment past his early series, without an anchor point to work from, generating chaotic evidence that identified him quickly. That argument holds. It held for Bundy. It did not hold for Samuel Little, and the reason it did not hold for Samuel Little is worth stating precisely, because it is not a contradiction of the pillar. It is a demonstration of what the pillar depends on to work.

The comfort zone protects an offender against local investigation by making him look like he belongs. Mobility ordinarily reverses that protection by making him look like a stranger. What Little demonstrates is that if the victim class is invisible in every jurisdiction, then being a stranger in every jurisdiction stops mattering. Nobody was looking for a linking pattern across states because nobody was looking for a linking pattern within any one state. His mobility was not what protected him. His victim selection was what protected him, and his mobility only mattered because it distributed the individually-invisible cases across a wide enough area that no one investigator or agency could have caught the pattern even if they had been looking.

Same variable, different operational consequence, because of what it interacts with. That is what the pillars actually do. They describe patterns whose meaning depends on the case as a whole, not on any one factor read in isolation.

How It Finally Broke

The way Little was caught is as instructive as the way he was missed, and it is a Los Angeles story, which is part of why it belongs in this book.

In September 2012, Little was arrested at a homeless shelter in Kentucky on a narcotics warrant and extradited to California. He was, at that point, a 72-year-old man in declining health, not obviously the most prolific killer in the country's history, just another name on a drug charge. What changed everything was that the Los Angeles Police Department obtained DNA in custody and connected it to three unsolved homicides from 1987 and 1989, the killings of women whose cases had gone cold years before.

The three cases were the murders of Carol Alford, killed July 13, 1987; Audrey Nelson, killed August 14, 1989; and Guadalupe Apodaca, killed

September 3, 1989. All three women had been strangled. All three had been dumped in alleys or abandoned buildings in South Los Angeles. None of the three cases had generated a suspect at the time, and each had gone cold in the ordinary way - worked hard for a period, then displaced by the next case, then filed.

The reason those files could speak again a quarter century later is that someone had done a specific piece of work in advance without knowing what it would eventually mean. When Audrey Nelson's body was examined in 1989, the officers noticed that she had scratched at her attacker, and they clipped and preserved the tissue under her fingernails. This was not standard practice in 1989. DNA collection under a homicide victim's fingernails as routine did not become the norm for several more years. The people who worked Nelson's scene that day did it anyway, because it was the disciplined thing to do, and because the object in front of them was clearly evidence whether or not there was yet a lab that could interpret it. That tissue sat in evidence for twenty-three years. In April 2012, when LAPD's cold case unit ran it through the CODIS offender database, it matched a man who had recently been arrested on an old warrant in Kentucky.

The whole case turned on a decision made in an alley in 1989 by a person doing his job carefully in the absence of any reason to think it would ever matter. That decision is the entire methodology of this book, compressed into a single act.

The detectives who built those cases were LAPD cold case investigators, among them Mitzi Roberts, Rick Jackson, and Tim Marcia. I mentioned Roberts a couple of chapters ago as an example of the kind of detective who keeps pulling files that the system is not pushing at her, and this is the case I had in mind. In November 2012, the DNA tied Little to the murder of Carol Alford. The team built three murder cases from the cold evidence, and in 2014 Little was convicted and sentenced to three consecutive life terms without the possibility of parole.

And that, in an ordinary case, would have been the end: three convictions, a life sentence, a file closed. What makes Little the defining case of the undercount problem is what happened next, because three convictions turned out to be the visible tip of ninety-three.

The Texas Ranger and the Confessions

The reason we know the true scale of Samuel Little is not forensic. It is testimonial, and it came years after his conviction, through a single investigator's patience.

Before Holland ever walked into an interview room, an FBI analyst named Christina Palazzolo had been building the case that Little was more than his three convictions.

Palazzolo works for the FBI's Violent Criminal Apprehension Program, ViCAP, which is the closest thing American law enforcement has to a system for the exact linkage problem Chapter 1 opened this book with. ViCAP's job is to look across jurisdictions at unsolved cases and identify ones that look like they might belong together. Working with Angela Williamson, a Department of Justice ViCAP liaison, Palazzolo had been running Little's known movement history against unsolved homicides in the states his records placed him in. One of the cases she found looked to her like him - a 1994 strangulation in Odessa, Texas, of a woman named Denise Brothers, whose body had been found partially clothed in a vacant lot, and whose case had gone cold in the ordinary way. Little's records placed him in Odessa around the time of the killing.

Palazzolo sent the lead to the Texas Rangers, because Odessa is Ranger territory. It landed on the desk of Ranger James Holland. That is the specific mechanism by which Holland got the interview access that eventually produced ninety-three confessions. It was not a lucky break, and it was not investigative genius on any one person's part. It was ViCAP doing the linkage work that no local agency could do alone, and it was Palazzolo specifically doing the pattern-recognition on a case whose profile matched an offender the system had, at that point, already caught. The convictions had happened. Nobody had yet asked what else Little might have done.

In 2018, a Texas Ranger named James Holland began interviewing Little in prison. Little, already serving three life terms with nothing left to lose and, by many accounts, a desire to be finally recognized for what he had done, began to talk. Over a series of interviews he confessed to 93 murders across the country, providing details, and in many cases drawing detailed portraits of his victims from memory. Those drawings, which the FBI later released publicly, became a tool for identification, haunting color portraits, mostly of Black women, offered to a public in the hope that someone would recognize a face that the system had never named.

What Holland did in those interviews is worth describing, because it is a piece of investigative technique that does not get taught much in the popular literature and that ran, in Little's case, directly against everything the popular literature says an interrogation is supposed to look like.

Holland spent more than seven hundred hours in interviews with Samuel Little across roughly two years. He did not push. He did not confront. He did not accuse. When Little talked, Holland listened. When Little wanted a transfer to a quieter facility in Texas - the Ector County jail was quieter than the LA County jail where Little was being held - Holland made it happen. When Little wanted to be listened to as the person who had done these things rather than as the person on trial for having done them, Holland gave him that too. Little, in his seventies and in declining health, serving three consecutive life sentences with nothing procedurally left to lose, had one thing he did want, and it was the thing every serial offender the popular literature describes wants at some point in his story. He wanted to be finally recognized for what he had done.

Holland gave him that recognition and, in exchange, Little began to talk. City by city, state by state. Jackson, Mississippi: one. Cincinnati, Ohio: one. Phoenix, Arizona: three. Las Vegas, Nevada: one. He gave descriptions of victims by physical detail, sometimes clothing, sometimes location where the body was left. He gave Holland the year, or the approximate year, and the season. Holland took it all down, and Palazzolo and Williamson worked from Washington to match each confession against the unsolved-homicide record.

This is not the interrogation model from the fiction. It is closer to the opposite of it. Holland is often referred to in the coverage as the serial killer whisperer, which is a piece of press branding I would not use, but the underlying observation is real. An offender who has nothing left to lose and something specific left to want can, given a patient and disciplined listener, become the most valuable witness in his own case. Nothing about that is comfortable. It is, nonetheless, the method that produced the record.

Sit with that for a moment, because it is the darkest confirmation of this book's argument. The most prolific serial killer in American history was, in the end, a more reliable source on his own victims than the investigative record was. He remembered them. He could describe where and when and what they looked like. The system that should have been accounting for them had, in case after case, recorded nothing, or recorded the wrong thing, so that decades later the way to identify the dead was to ask the man who killed them to draw their faces. That is what an undercount looks like when you finally turn around and measure it. It looks like a murderer's sketchbook doing the work that fifty years of case files should have done.

Some of the portraits have been identified. Some have not. As of the last public updates, sixty-two of Little's confessed victims have been named. That number will probably continue to rise. Some of it will not.

Sit with the shape of that for a moment. In the specific cases the FBI could not close by ordinary forensic means, the identification of the victim came from the killer. He had a better record of who these women were than the system that was supposed to be tracking their deaths did. He drew their faces from memory decades after killing them; the system had never even written their names down.

That is the sentence this chapter has been building toward, and it is the sentence the entire book has been building toward, and I want it stated plainly before we move on. The most prolific serial killer in the recorded history of the United States was, in the end, a more reliable source on the existence of his own victims than the police reports and coroners' files of nineteen states across thirty-five years. That is not a claim about Samuel Little. It is a claim about the machinery that was supposed to catch him, and about what the machinery did not count.

What Little Proves

Every methodological thread in this book runs through Samuel Little, and I want to draw them together here, because this is the case where they stop being separate lessons and become a single argument.

The linkage problem from Chapter 1: Little is its largest instance, made unsolvable for decades not because the cases were hard to link but because many were never recorded as cases to link. The comfort zone from Chapter 4: Little shows that the zone need not be geographic at all, that it can be a category of victim rather than a place, and that this kind of zone is far more dangerous because it does not show up on any map an analyst could draw. Victim selection from Chapter 2: Little is the framework's most extreme illustration, an offender who read the system's priorities correctly and hunted in the exact space the system had left unattended. And the human cost from Chapter 6: the detectives who finally broke him were cold case investigators doing the work of assembling what the system had scattered, one file at a time, decades late.

But Little proves one more thing, and it is the thing I most want a reader to take from this chapter. The reason he was able to kill ninety-three people was not that he was extraordinary. By every measure this book has applied, he was ordinary: average in the ways Chapter 3 described, mobile in a way that should have exposed him, reliant on no genius and no elaborate method, just a pair of hands and a reliable supply of victims nobody was counting. What was extraordinary was the size of the blind spot he found. He is not a testament to the capability of serial killers. He is a testament to the cost of not looking, measured in the only unit that matters, which is human lives, at least ninety-three of them, and very likely more, most of whom we still cannot name.

The methodology in this book works. Samuel Little is the proof of what happens when it is not applied, when the pattern is never assembled because the individual pieces were never valued enough to be written down. He believed no one was accounting for his victims. The whole purpose of the discipline this book describes is to make sure that belief is never again correct.

The methodology this book has described exists specifically to close that gap, and it does not close it primarily through better forensics. It closes it by treating every missing person as a case to be linked, by treating every unattributed death as a case that belongs to a series until proven otherwise, by treating every triage decision as a decision that has downstream consequences for the offender it is, at that moment, quietly protecting.

Samuel Little died in a California prison in December 2020. Ranger James Holland retired from the Texas Rangers a few years later. Christina

Palazzolo continued at ViCAP. The identifications of Little's victims are still, at the time of this writing, incomplete. Cases are still being matched. Some never will be.

If the discipline this book has argued for did not exist, none of Little's ninety-three would ever have been counted. That the number is now available to be counted is the argument. That thirty-one of them may never be given a name is the counter-argument. Both are true, both are permanent, and the practitioner's job is to hold both in view and keep working.

ON THE RECORD

Established

- **Samuel Little is the most prolific serial killer in U.S.** history. He confessed to 93 murders between 1970 and 2005; the FBI has confirmed at least 50, later 60, and considers all 93 confessions credible.
- **Many of his killings were never recorded as homicides.** Victims' deaths were frequently ruled overdoses, accidents, or undetermined; some bodies were never found. There was often no case file to link.
- **His comfort zone was a category of victim, not a place.** He was mobile across many states, which usually exposes an offender. He survived it by preying on people the system was not counting.
- **The case broke on cold-case forensic work.** LAPD obtained DNA in 2012 linking him to three 1980s homicides; cold case detectives built the cases that led to three life sentences in 2014.

Myth

- **That the most prolific killer must be a criminal genius.** Little was ordinary by every measure in this book. What was extraordinary was the size of the blind spot he exploited, not the man.

- **That mobility protects a killer.** It usually does the opposite. Little got away with it only because his victim selection made each killing individually invisible.

What the record shows

- **The killer became a better record than the system.** Little identified victims from memory and drew their portraits, which the FBI used to try to name the dead the case files never had.
- **He believed no one was accounting for his victims.** For most of thirty-five years, he was right. That sentence is the entire argument of this book, stated by the offender.

Chapter 10: Zodiac and the Performative Signature

The pillars work when the offender cannot help producing them.

That sentence has been implicit throughout this book, and it is time to state it explicitly, because this chapter is about the case where the sentence stops being true, and the methodology hits its clearest limit.

Chapter 4 defined signature as a ritual element that is not necessary to complete the crime, present because the offender needs it to be. Chapter 6 showed BTK undone by exactly that need - Rader could not stop feeding his signature, and the floppy disk was the medium the compulsion eventually chose. The general pattern the methodology depends on is that signature is involuntary. The offender does not decide to leave it. He does not decide how much of it to leave. He does not decide when to stop leaving it. That involuntariness is what makes signature the specific piece of evidence that identifies an offender across scenes, because he is not in a position to withhold it or vary it strategically.

Now consider what happens when an offender deliberately produces a signature-like body of material, controls its distribution, releases it on his own terms, and stops when he chooses. That is a different thing. It has the surface features of signature - repetition, personal style, elements not required by the crime - and none of the diagnostic properties, because at every step it reflects a choice rather than a compulsion.

The Zodiac case is the paradigm example of this in the American record, and it is worth saying at the outset why it belongs in this book despite not having been solved. The methodology this book describes has limits. This chapter is one of them, made visible.

What the Record Documents

Before anything else, a note on what this chapter treats as factual and what it does not.

The Zodiac case has generated more secondary literature, more competing suspect claims, and more contested attribution than any other unsolved American serial murder case. Across five and a half decades, dozens of individuals have been publicly named as suspects, in books, in documentaries, in film treatments, in press releases from amateur investigative groups, and in personal accounts by people who believed they had identified the offender. Some of these accusations have received substantial media attention. Some have been the basis of best-selling books. Some have been presented with what their authors regard as conclusive circumstantial evidence.

As of the writing of this chapter, no identification of the offender has been established to the evidentiary standard required for prosecution. The case has had official suspects - the SFPD and the joint task force have investigated specific individuals formally over the years - but each has been excluded, or has failed to be confirmed, by the physical evidence available. The FBI's San Francisco division still lists the case as an ongoing investigation. The San Francisco Police Department has declined to close it despite periodic announcements from outside groups claiming to have solved it.

That gap - between the number of proposed identifications and the number of evidentiary confirmations - is not incidental to what this chapter is about. It is close to the central point. The physical evidence in the case has been the check on the claims, not the other way around. Fingerprints recovered at the Presidio Heights scene have been compared against exemplars from every named suspect. DNA testing on the letter adhesives has been attempted repeatedly as the technology has matured. Handwriting comparisons have been run against known writing samples from every seriously proposed candidate. That check has applied equally to the identifications proposed by outside researchers and to the persons of interest developed by the investigating agencies themselves. The evidence, in every case that has come to a decision point, has declined to confirm.

That is the discipline this book has been describing throughout. The evidence is the arbiter. A story about who the offender might have been, however plausible, however emotionally satisfying, does not become an identification until the physical evidence bears it out. In the Zodiac case, for reasons this chapter will get to, the physical evidence has consistently declined to bear any of them out.

This chapter names no suspects, endorses no attribution, and cites no popular treatment as a source for facts. The material below is drawn from the documented record: contemporary case files, published forensic reports, court records, the FBI's public releases, and the letters and ciphers whose authenticity has been established by the joint SFPD/FBI Zodiac task force. Where the record is contested - as it is on several matters that popular sources treat as settled - this chapter says so.

That constraint is not incidental. It is closer to the point of the chapter, because a case in which the offender's identity remains disputed after fifty-five years produces exactly the kind of literature in which one unsourced claim borrows credibility from another until the whole picture becomes impossible to check. The discipline is to work only from what can be checked.

The Confirmed Attacks

Between December 1968 and October 1969, five people were killed and two were seriously injured in a series of attacks in the San Francisco Bay Area that were subsequently connected to a single offender through ballistic evidence, physical evidence, eyewitness accounts, and the offender's own claims of responsibility.

The first attack occurred on the night of December 20, 1968, on Lake Herman Road outside Benicia. Betty Lou Jensen, sixteen, and David Faraday, seventeen, were shot at close range as they sat in a parked car. Both were killed.

The second occurred on July 4, 1969, at Blue Rock Springs Park in Vallejo. Darlene Ferrin, twenty-two, and Michael Mageau, nineteen, were shot as they sat in a parked car. Ferrin was killed. Mageau was seriously wounded and survived. Ballistic analysis subsequently matched the rounds recovered from the Blue Rock Springs scene to those recovered from Lake Herman Road, establishing that both attacks were committed with the same firearm. Shortly after the second attack, an unknown male made a phone call to the Vallejo Police Department claiming responsibility for both.

The third occurred on September 27, 1969, at Lake Berryessa, in Napa County. Bryan Hartnell, twenty, and Cecelia Shepard, twenty-two, were attacked while picnicking at the lakeshore. The offender approached them wearing a hooded costume with a symbol on the chest, tied them, and stabbed them repeatedly. Shepard died of her injuries two days later. Hartnell survived. Before leaving the scene, the offender wrote in black felt-tip pen on the door of Hartnell's car: three dates corresponding to the previous attacks, the words "by knife," and a distinctive symbol - a circle divided by a cross.

The fourth occurred on the night of October 11, 1969, in the Presidio Heights neighborhood of San Francisco. Paul Stine, twenty-nine, a taxi driver, was shot in the head in the front seat of his cab at the corner of Washington and Cherry Streets. Three teenage witnesses in a house across the street saw the offender leave the cab, wipe surfaces down, and walk away in the direction of the Presidio. Their description became the basis for the composite sketch that would circulate publicly for the next fifty-five years.

Two survivors. Five dead. Four scenes, three linked by ballistics, one linked by eyewitness identification and physical evidence. That is the confirmed body of the case. Every other victim attribution made in the popular literature - and there are several, some of which have been treated as settled fact by researchers over the decades - remains disputed, and this chapter treats them as such.

The Communications

Four days after the third attack, on October 15, 1969, the offender's identity as a single perpetrator of a documented series became a matter of public record in a way no serial homicide investigation in the United States had previously experienced.

The offender began writing to the newspapers.

Between July 1969 and 1974, the San Francisco Chronicle, the San Francisco Examiner, the Vallejo Times-Herald, attorney Melvin Belli, and several other recipients received a series of letters, cards, and coded messages from a person calling himself Zodiac. The offender claimed responsibility for the confirmed attacks and, in later letters, for additional killings the police were unable to verify. He included details of the crimes that were not public at the time of the letters, which the task force treated as confirmation of authorship. He signed the letters with the same crossed-circle symbol left at the Lake Berryessa scene.

The letters were extraordinary in several respects. They were literate, though with a distinctive spelling pattern the task force analysts recognized across correspondence. They contained coded messages - ciphers built from a mixed alphabet of symbols, punctuation, letters, and shapes. They included threats of specific future actions. They included taunts about the police investigation. They included one death threat against a specific school bus of children, which the offender did not act on but which caused Bay Area law enforcement to protect school routes for years.

The first cipher, three parts totaling four hundred and eight characters, was sent to the three Bay Area newspapers on July 31, 1969. It was solved eight days later by Donald and Bettye Harden, a Salinas schoolteacher and his wife who worked on the puzzle at home. The decrypted message was ideological, angry, and grandiose. It did not identify the offender.

A second cipher, three hundred and forty characters, was sent to the Chronicle on November 8, 1969. It resisted every attempt at solution - professional, amateur, cryptographic-academic - for fifty-one years. On December 5, 2020, three independent codebreakers, David Oranchak in the United States, Sam Blake in Australia, and Jarl Van Eycke in Belgium, submitted a solution to the FBI's Cryptanalysis and Racketeering Records Unit. The solution was confirmed as valid. The decrypted message was, again, taunting and self-referential. The offender wrote that he hoped his pursuers were having fun trying to catch him and that he was not afraid of the gas chamber. It did not identify him.

The letters diminished in frequency through the 1970s and stopped. The last communication generally accepted as authentic by the task force was sent in 1974. There have been letters and calls claiming to be Zodiac since, in every decade. None have been authenticated.

What the Communications Were Doing

Set the communications against the definition of signature from Chapter 4, and something specific becomes visible.

A signature, in the Douglas sense the book has used, is a ritual element present at the scene of the crime, not necessary to complete it, and reflecting a psychological need the offender cannot fully suppress. The Lake Berryessa costume and the crossed-circle symbol drawn on Hartnell's car door meet that definition. They were unnecessary to the killing, they were present because the offender needed them to be, and they were consistent with material the offender was producing elsewhere. That is signature in the normal sense.

The letters are a different category. They were not left at scenes. They were produced afterward, at a remove, at the offender's convenience, in a form he chose and sent to recipients he selected. They contained material he decided to include and omitted material he decided to withhold. When he wanted the cipher to be difficult, he made it difficult. When he wanted to include a taunt, he included a taunt. When he wanted to stop, he stopped. The signature-like properties of the letters - the crossed-circle symbol, the ideology, the linguistic tics, the escalation and de-escalation - reflect at every point choices the offender was in a position to make.

That is what a staged signature is, and it behaves differently from a compulsive one.

A compulsive signature identifies the offender because he cannot help producing it, cannot help varying it inside a stable envelope, and cannot help continuing to produce it after the killings stop. Rader's signature is the paradigm case. He communicated for decades, and when he tried to stop he could not, and the communication is what caught him. A staged signature, by contrast, produces exactly what the offender wants it to produce, includes exactly the elements he wants included, and stops when he decides it is time to stop. It looks like signature. It behaves like performance.

The distinction matters operationally. Every diagnostic property of signature that Chapter 4 identified as useful to the investigation depends on the offender's inability to modulate it. When the offender can and does modulate it, those properties do not appear. He can withhold his identity. He can vary his style deliberately to defeat linguistic analysis. He can stop and start on a schedule that has nothing to do with any inner compulsion an investigator could read.

The Zodiac case is the demonstration of what an investigation of a maximally-staged signature looks like. The material is voluminous. The material is stylistically distinctive. The material is confirmed as authored by the same person. And none of it, across fifty-five years, has produced an identification.

The Cost of Speculation

There is a further piece of this that belongs in the chapter, because it is a specific mechanism by which the case has stayed unsolved that goes beyond the argument about signature. The Zodiac offender's staging did not only produce material designed not to identify him. It produced a case, in the culture, that has generated more independent claims of identification than any other unsolved American serial murder investigation, and each of them has required official work to disprove.

The general fact is well-documented, and it is worth stating in general terms rather than cataloguing specific instances. Many people have confessed to being the Zodiac; the record of these confessions goes back to the first year of the case and has continued in every decade since. Many identifications have been proposed by researchers who believed they had solved the case. Some of these have been published in books, some in documentaries, some as press releases. None has been forensically established to the standard a criminal prosecution would require. That much can be said accurately without walking through any specific candidate, and this chapter is not going to walk through any specific candidate. Adjudicating individual claims is other people's work, some of it done responsibly and some not, and stepping into that adjudication would put this book into a debate whose merits it cannot resolve.

The methodological point, though, does belong here. Every claim of identification that reaches the investigation with enough specificity to be checked has to be checked. This is not optional work. Fingerprint comparison against the Presidio Heights print. Handwriting comparison against the letter exemplars. Where the person is deceased and the family cooperates, or where records can be obtained, DNA comparison against material recovered from letter adhesives. Records searches to confirm or exclude the person's presence in the Bay Area during the confirmed attack window. Interviews with anyone who might place the person or exclude them from placement. Each of these tasks takes work.

Not enormous work, in any single instance. But cumulatively, across decades of proposed identifications, substantial. And the total is not the point. The distribution is. Investigators work under triage, which this book has said before and will keep saying because it is the material condition under which all of this happens. Every hour spent on a lead is an hour not spent on another. When a substantial fraction of investigative time on an open case is directed by claims arriving from outside the case, rather than by evidence generated by the investigation itself, the work becomes reactive rather than proactive. That is not necessarily bad, and it is not the fault of the investigators, and it is not something they can refuse to do without abandoning the case. But it does describe the case's condition accurately, and the condition has costs.

Here is where the argument connects to Chapter 1 in a way I want to make explicit. Chapter 1 established that linkage is the entire methodological problem of serial murder investigation, and that linkage runs on evidence, not on plausibility. Investigators developed a specific operational technique for handling exactly the situation this section is describing, and it is a technique that predates the Zodiac case and applies far beyond it. They withhold specific case details. They do not release, publicly or across jurisdictions, particular facts about a crime scene that only the offender could know. When a confessor arrives, or a proposed identification arrives with corroborating detail attached, the investigators check whether the detail includes the withheld facts. If it does, the claim becomes credible. If it does not, the claim is excluded, because a person confessing to a crime he did not commit cannot know the facts that were never made public.

This is the operational solution to the false-confession problem, and it is not an accident that it looks structurally like the linkage argument. Withheld details serve the same function as unshared signature details do in a linkage: they are the evidence that only the offender could provide, and their presence or absence in a claim determines whether the claim is worth pursuing. The Grim Sleeper investigation, which is the subject of the next chapter, was worked in exactly this way for exactly this reason - specific facts of the earlier scenes were held back from the public record for decades, precisely so that when the offender was eventually identified through familial DNA, the corroboration would still be available and the linkage would still be defensible. Zodiac and Grim Sleeper are the same problem, worked with the same tool, ending in opposite outcomes.

That is the discipline the investigation has been running under, and it is the discipline that has excluded the identifications proposed over the decades. The physical record contains facts that the outside claims have consistently failed to reproduce. The investigators have not confirmed any of the identifications not because they are being stubborn about it, and not because they are protecting turf, but because the standard the withheld-detail method sets has not been met by any of the candidates proposed. When it is met, the case will move. Until it is met, the case will stay where it is.

Which brings the argument back around to where the section started. The offender's staging did not only defeat the signature diagnostic. It also, indirectly and probably without his ever intending to, generated a case whose external attention has produced an investigative workload that could not have existed for a lower-profile case, and that workload has been necessarily reactive because the alternative - dismissing outside claims without checking them - would have been indefensible. That the workload has consistently failed to produce a confirmed identification is not because the investigators have been careless. It is because the withheld-detail method is doing exactly what it was designed to do, and the standard it sets is one that no proposed identification has yet met.

He is protected, in other words, by the same disciplines that protect the case from being falsely closed. That is a symmetric situation, and it is worth stating symmetrically. The methodology that will eventually identify him, if he is ever identified, will be the same methodology that has kept every wrong identification from being adopted. This chapter's argument about the limits of the framework does not extend to a claim that the framework has failed. It extends only to the observation that the framework, applied honestly, does not currently produce an identification, and will not until evidence appears that meets the standard the withheld-detail method requires.

What the Physical Evidence Did

Notice which parts of the Zodiac case have moved and which have not, because the pattern says something the popular literature usually misses.

The scenes themselves produced the ordinary output of homicide investigation. Ballistic matches connected the first two attacks. Physical evidence at Lake Berryessa - the shoe prints, the handwriting on the car door - connected the third attack to the first two. Eyewitness identification at Presidio Heights connected the fourth attack to the composite sketch, which the offender himself later criticized in a letter, effectively confirming that the sketch resembled him. Fingerprints were recovered at Presidio Heights. Handwriting on the envelopes and letters was compared against known exemplars. DNA testing has been attempted on adhesive from stamps and envelopes as the technology has matured.

None of this material has identified the offender either.

The letters have moved further than the scenes have. The second cipher was solved in 2020. The Presidio Heights fingerprint has been compared against exemplars for fifty-five years. The letter material is periodically re-examined against updated DNA technology. Each of these efforts extends the physical record slightly. None of them has closed the gap between the record and the identification.

What the case demonstrates is that the ordinary tools of homicide investigation are sufficient to establish a series and insufficient to identify an offender who has organized his signature to be non-diagnostic. The pillars still describe what the offender did. Chapter 4's comfort zone: the attacks clustered in the Bay Area, with a specific geographic and cultural corridor Zodiac appeared to know. Chapter 4's victim selection: young couples in isolated locations, a taxi driver working alone at night - victims who could be approached without a network of witnesses being available. Chapter 4's trophies: none recovered, because there is no offender to have searched.

Chapter 4's signature: present, elaborate, extensively communicated, and inert for identification purposes.

The pillars describe the case accurately. They do not identify the offender. That is not a failure of the pillars. It is a demonstration of a specific structural feature of the framework that this chapter is here to name: the pillars identify offenders when the pillars produce diagnostic information. When one pillar, particularly signature, is being run by an offender who understands what signature does and controls it deliberately, that pillar's diagnostic yield drops toward zero, and the investigation is left working from the others alone. In the Zodiac case, the others were not sufficient.

The Ongoing Case

The case remains open. That sentence is worth ending the chapter on for a specific reason, because it means the analysis in this chapter is potentially incomplete in a way none of the analyses in the previous case chapters can be.

Every open investigation might close. DNA technology continues to advance. Familial DNA - the technique that will be central to the next chapter - was not available for most of the Zodiac case's history and has been applied selectively to the surviving physical evidence with limited results, so far. If the offender's identity is ever established, the analysis in this chapter will need to be revisited to see whether it survives contact with facts that are not currently in the record. My honest expectation is that the argument survives - that if the offender is ever identified, we will find a person whose signature was as deliberately constructed as the record suggests, not one whose signature was compulsive in a way we have failed to read. But an honest practitioner cannot rule out being wrong, and I want to say so before the chapter closes.

What is certain, and what does not depend on eventual identification, is the methodological point the case establishes. Not every signature is diagnostic. The framework depends on offenders producing material they cannot help producing, and offenders who are producing material they choose to produce look superficially similar and behave completely differently. The distinction is one the discipline has to hold onto, because when an investigator confuses the two, the case receives an enormous amount of attention and no progress.

Fifty-five years of Zodiac investigation is what that confusion looks like at scale. The offender has stayed hidden not because the pillars fail as a general framework, but because a specific kind of offender, aware of what he is doing and deliberate about what he releases, can neutralize the specific pillar that ordinarily does the most work. That should not be encouraging news for offenders reading this book. Deliberate staging on the Zodiac scale requires a level of discipline and self-suppression that is not sustainable across large series, which is why the Zodiac series stopped where it did. The offender chose absence over recognition, and absence is what he got.

The chapter closes on that, because it is the honest thing to say. Some cases the discipline does not solve. The reason has to do with what the specific offender chose to be, and the recognition of that pattern is itself part of the methodology.

ON THE RECORD

Established

- **The Zodiac case documents at least five deaths and two survivors across four confirmed attacks in the Bay Area between December 1968 and October 1969.** The attacks were connected through ballistic matches, physical evidence, eyewitness identification, and the offender's own communications.
- **The offender produced a large and stylistically distinctive body of communications between 1969 and 1974.** The letters and ciphers are authenticated as being from a single author. Two of the four ciphers have been solved - the first by the Hardens in 1969, the second by Oranchak, Blake, and Van Eycke in 2020.
- **The case remains unsolved as of this writing.** The FBI's San Francisco division continues to list it as active. No identification of the offender has been established to the evidentiary standard required for prosecution. The case has had official suspects across

the decades; each has been excluded, or has failed to be confirmed, by the physical evidence available.

- **A deliberately staged signature is a different diagnostic object than a compulsive one.** Signature identifies an offender when he cannot help producing it; when he can and does control it, the pillar's diagnostic yield drops to zero and the case has to be worked from the other pillars alone.
- **The false-confession problem and the linkage problem are solved with the same tool.** Withheld case details serve the same function in filtering false confessions that unshared signature details serve in confirming a linkage. The physical evidence is the arbiter in both.

Myth

- **That the Zodiac case has been solved.** It has not. Every announcement to the contrary has failed to produce an official confirmation, and this book takes no position on any named suspect.
- **That the signature material would have identified the offender if only it had been read correctly.** It would not have. A staged signature is designed to be visible without being diagnostic, and no amount of stylistic or cryptographic analysis substitutes for physical evidence that connects material to a person.
- **That the case's persistence reflects any specific failure of the investigating agencies.** It reflects the structural limit of a methodology when applied to an offender who understood what signature was and deliberately produced material with the surface features and none of the diagnostic properties.

Still unsettled

- **The offender's identity.** This may be resolved by future DNA analysis of preserved physical evidence. It may not be.
- **The extent of the offender's true series.** He claimed a much higher body count in his letters. The task force treats those claims as unverified. Whether any of the disputed attributions belong in

the confirmed record awaits evidence the record does not currently contain.

- **Whether the analysis in this chapter survives eventual identification.** If the offender is identified, whether the person turns out to have been running a deliberately staged signature, as this chapter argues, or a compulsive signature that the analysis has misread, will be a question the identification will answer. I have named my expectation and reserved the right to be wrong.

Chapter 11: The Grim Sleeper and the Room Behind the Wall

This is the case the prologue of this book opened with, and it is the case this book has been circling from the first page. It is also the one I was closest to. I want to tell it in order, from the killings forward to the closure, because the order is where the lessons live. The methodology this book has spent ten chapters describing was applied, in this case, to a series that ran for a quarter of a century, and every pillar the earlier chapters named shows up in it. Comfort zone. Victim selection. Trophies. The signature that survives a change of method. And, at the end, the piece of evidence that finally did the thing the whole discipline exists to do, which is to connect a body found in an alley in 1985 to a man arrested at his home in 2010.

I was the lead photographer on the search of that home. I will get to the room behind the wall, because it is why the prologue exists. But the room is near the end of the story, and the story starts twenty-five years earlier, with women who were being killed in South Los Angeles and were not being connected to one another.

The Killings, and the Gap That Was Not a Gap

The killings began in the mid-1980s, in the neighborhoods along and around Western Avenue in South Los Angeles. The first confirmed victim, Debra Jackson, was found in an alley in August 1985. Over the next three years, more women were found in similar circumstances, in the same few square miles, most of them shot with a small-caliber pistol. Then, by the accounting that would later give the case its name, the killings appeared to stop. For over a decade, no murders were being linked to the same offender. Then, in the early 2000s, women began being found again in the same area, killed in the same corridor, and the series that had seemed to end picked back up. The last confirmed victim, Janecia Peters, was found on the first day of 2007.

The arithmetic of the case needs to be stated carefully, in the same three tiers I used for Samuel Little, because the difference between the tiers is the whole point of a book about linkage. Franklin was convicted of ten counts of first-degree murder and one count of attempted murder. The cases officially linked to him number more than forty. My own recollection, from the years I was near this investigation, is that the true figure is nearly twice that. I state those as three different kinds of claim, because they are three different kinds of claim. The ten are proven beyond a reasonable doubt. The more than forty are linked by evidence. The rest is my recollection, and I mark it as such.

Why He Was Called the Grim Sleeper

The name came from the gap, and the name is wrong in a way that teaches the central lesson of this book, so it is worth slowing down on.

In August 2008, an L.A. Weekly reporter named Christine Pelisek broke the story that a serial killer who had been active in the 1980s was active again, and had been for years, in South Los Angeles. She and her editor gave him a name, the Grim Sleeper, because of the apparent fourteen-year hiatus in his killings, from 1988 to 2002. The name stuck. The LAPD adopted it. It is the name on the true-crime books and the documentaries and the billboard that would later go up asking the public for help. Pelisek deserves the credit for the name and for a great deal more; her reporting is a substantial reason the case got the attention it eventually did.

But the name describes something that did not happen. He did not sleep. Here is what actually happened, and it is the difference between what the police could see and what the offender did.

A serial killer working South Los Angeles in the 1980s was not, in those years, being tracked as a single offender. Several unsolved killers were operating in the same part of the city in that era, and the cases were being worked, when they were worked, under a catch-all name that lumped more than one offender together. My own opinion, and I state it as opinion, is that giving several separate offenders one shared external name had the effect, intended or not, of obscuring how many distinct serial killers were actually operating in that area at that time. There was more than one serial killer in South Los Angeles in those years. This is the most famous of them.

The task force that had been chasing the 1985-to-1988 killings was disbanded in 1988. For more than a decade after that, there was no dedicated team left to connect the bodies that kept appearing. Women were still being found. They were simply not being linked to one another, because linking cold cases across years takes a dedicated effort, and the dedicated effort had been dissolved. When detectives finally reviewed the cold cases years later, the Los Angeles Times counted roughly eleven additional murders in the gap years that Franklin could have committed. Prosecutors named further possible victims, including one who died around 2000. He was not tried for any of these. The senior investigators on the case, Detective Dennis Kilcoyne and Detective Daryn Dupree among them, are on record that he never truly stopped.

So the sleep was a detection gap, not a behavioral one. The name describes what the police could see, which was an absence of linked cases. It does not describe what the offender did, which was to keep killing while no one was connecting the evidence.

There is a second reason the two clusters of killings looked like the work of two different people, and it is the exact distinction this book drew several chapters ago between method and signature. The early victims were shot with a .25 caliber pistol. The later cluster included victims who were strangled, among them Princess Berthomieux and Valerie McCorvey. To anyone reading the surface of the crimes, a shooter and a strangler are two different offenders. The method had changed. The how had changed.

What had not changed was everything underneath the method. The same victim profile. The same few square miles. And, above all, the physical evidence. The read I got from the detectives, which I pass along as their read and not as anything in the public record, was that his pattern shifted during the middle years because he was raising his son. That is a motive claim, it sits outside the evidence, and the case does not need it, so I set it down here and move on. What matters is what tied the clusters together, and it was not the method. It was Detective Cliff Shepard matching DNA from one of the earliest victims to the two newer murders, with the 1988 ballistics tying in behind it. The moment the DNA connected an early victim to the later cluster, the sleep evaporated. There had never been a sleep. There had been one offender, changing his method, across a detection gap that looked like silence and was not.

That is the signature-versus-method lesson from Chapter 4, living inside a single case. The method is the how, and it adapts. The signature and the physical evidence are what survive the adaptation, and they are what let you prove that one hand was behind crimes that looked like the work of several.

The Break

By the time the case had a name and a task force again, the investigation had crime-scene DNA from multiple victims and no one to match it to. Franklin had never been in the system in a way that mattered. He had no felony conviction that would have placed his own DNA in the database. Under the ordinary way these searches work, a crime-scene profile is run against the database of known offenders, and if the offender is not in the database, the search comes back empty. It came back empty.

Two pieces of public scaffolding matter here. In 2004, California voters passed Proposition 69, which expanded the collection of DNA from convicted felons. For the purposes of this book, the important thing about a DNA profile is that the law treats it as a biological identifier, on the same footing as an older biological marker like a fingerprint. It identifies a person. In April 2008, California enacted a familial DNA search program, the first of its kind in any state in the country. A familial search does something the ordinary search cannot. Instead of asking whether the crime-scene profile matches anyone in the database exactly, it asks whether the profile is a close-but-imperfect match to someone in the database, close in the specific way that a parent and child, or two siblings, resemble each other genetically. A near match is not the offender. It is a member of the offender's family.

The first familial search under the new California program was run in November 2008, and its target was the Grim Sleeper. It failed. There was no relative of the offender in the database yet. That is worth sitting with for a moment, because it is the kind of detail that shows how contingent these things are. They went looking for him with the new tool, first, before anyone else, and the tool came back empty for a reason that had nothing to do with the tool. The relative it needed was not yet in the system.

He entered the system the next year. Franklin's son, Christopher Franklin, was convicted of a felony weapons charge in 2009, and his DNA was collected and entered into the state databank for the first time. When the state ran a familial search again in 2010, the crime-scene profile came back as a partial match to Christopher. The match was too close to ignore and too imperfect to be the man himself. Christopher was far too young to have committed murders in the 1980s. But a partial match of that kind points down a bloodline, and the bloodline pointed at a male relative of the right age. That relative was Christopher's father, Lonnie David Franklin Jr., who lived in the very part of South Los Angeles where the victims had been found.

It is worth being precise about what this case was, because the precision is the landmark. The Grim Sleeper case was the first time a familial DNA database search identified a serial killer and led to a murder conviction in the United States. It was not the first familial DNA search in the country; an earlier search in Denver in 2008, in a property crime, predates it. What made this one a landmark was the crime. A serial murderer was identified through his son's DNA, and the identification held up all the way to a conviction. The California Attorney General's office, announcing the arrest, called it an unprecedented use of familial DNA, and on the specific thing that made it matter, that description was accurate.

The technique was not a one-off. Seven years later, familial DNA tied a man named Geovanni Borjas to the 2011 murders of Michelle Lozano and Bree'Anna Guzman, and he was arrested in 2017; the LAPD described it as the second time the technique had led the department to a high-profile killer, the first being the Grim Sleeper. It is worth noting, to keep the methods straight, that the later and more famous genetic-genealogy cases, the ones that identified the Golden State Killer and others by building family trees out of consumer ancestry databases, are a different technique from what caught Franklin. Franklin was caught by a search of a law-enforcement database for a close biological relative already convicted of a crime. The door that opened here was a specific one, and it opened first on this case.

The Surveillance, and the Sample

A partial familial match is a lead, not a case. To confirm that Lonnie Franklin was the source of the crime-scene DNA, the investigation needed a direct sample of Franklin's own DNA, and it needed to obtain it without alerting him, because a man who knows he is being tested for a capital series of murders is a man who runs. The Metropolitan Division of the LAPD placed Franklin under round-the-clock surveillance.

During that surveillance, there was a night that has stayed with the people who worked it. Franklin picked up a woman. The team watching him understood, given what they believed he had done, that they might be watching the opening of another murder. They also could not move without risking the entire operation and, with it, the evidence that could convict him. He did not harm her. The surveillance held. I include this not for drama but because it is the true weight of that kind of work; the people on that detail carried the possibility, for the length of a night, that restraint might cost a life, and they were right to hold, and it did not, and both of those facts are true at once and neither cancels the other.

The sample, when it came, came from a search warrant and a discarded piece of food. On July 5, 2010, Franklin attended a family birthday party at a pizzeria in Orange County. An undercover officer worked the event as a busboy. When Franklin finished eating and left, the officer collected an item he had discarded, a pizza crust in the account I know, and segregated it cleanly so the sample would not be contaminated by anyone else's biological material. The item went to the lab. DNA turnaround at that time ran roughly three weeks, though this was expedited. The profile from the discarded food matched the crime-scene evidence. On July 7, 2010, Lonnie David Franklin Jr. was arrested at his home, and the search of the house began.

The Room Behind the Wall

This is the part the prologue promised.

The house was an ordinary South Los Angeles house, and the garage was an ordinary cluttered garage, and inside the garage was a space that was not ordinary. Someone had built a concealed room. It had no windows. It had a makeshift door. And the inside of it, in contrast to the disorder of the garage around it, was noticeably neat, kept in a way the rest of the space was not.

I want to describe what that concealment looked like to a professional eye, because the popular imagination of a hidden room like this runs immediately to criminal genius, and that is not what I saw. It read less like sophistication and more like mimicry. It read like a man who had absorbed the tropes of serial-killer movies and was imitating them, building the thing the films had told him a man like him was supposed to have, the place where one hides the trophies. That is a description of what the concealment communicated, and I offer it as a professional impression and nothing more.

My title at the time was Senior Photographer II. My role on this scene was Lead Photographer. On the search of that house I went into the concealed room to look it over and to give some light direction to the photographer who was documenting it, less because the direction was needed, since the field photographers were fully capable of the work, and more as the ordinary supervisory diligence of the role, the dotting of i's and the crossing of t's on a scene where every image would eventually matter. Detective Cliff Shepard, whose DNA match had broken the linkage years earlier, was present. The photographer documenting the space did the actual work of recording it. What that room contained, and what it eventually connected, is the subject the rest of this book has been building toward, and it is the reason the prologue exists. A concealed archive is worth more to a man like Franklin than the weapon that produced it. That is the trophy principle from Chapter 4, made physical, inside a wall, in a garage, in the neighborhood where the killings had happened.

Ten of Many

Only ten cases were taken to trial, though the evidence linked far more, and the reason is a piece of prosecutorial strategy that I heard explained to the families in my own presence.

The reasoning was this. Trying ten cases first, rather than forty, meant that if any single conviction were ever overturned on appeal, the prosecution would still be holding a large reserve of additional charges it had not yet brought. They could charge the next set immediately, and the next, and the next. The strategy ensured that no appellate reversal could ever result in Franklin walking free, because there would always be another set of provable murders waiting. Ten was not a ceiling on what he had done. Ten was a floor built deliberately low enough to be certain and deep enough to be permanent.

That is the place to set the three tiers of the count beside one another one last time. Ten convictions. More than forty officially linked. My own recollection of nearly twice that. Franklin was convicted, and on August 10, 2016, he was sentenced to death.

The Room With the Families

Before the first trial, I was present at the notifications to the victims' families. I was not told in advance why I was there.

What I came to understand, sitting in that room, was the specific reason the forensic staff had been brought in. We were civilians, not police. We were introduced to the families as the people who had gathered the evidence against Franklin and had made sure it was gathered properly. In a community whose trust in the police had been worn thin by exactly the kind of neglect that had let this series run for a quarter of a century, the forensic staff were trusted for a reason the police sometimes were not. We were the people who had done the technical work, and the technical work was the thing that had finally, unambiguously, named the man.

The room held real sorrow. It was uncomfortable to sit inside that grief, and I am not going to pretend otherwise or dress it up. But it also gave me something I have kept. It gave me the sense that the forensic side had done its part in delivering closure to people who had waited, some of them, for twenty-five years. There is a distinction I hold onto from that work, and it matters. Forensic professionals want the killer caught. Not a killer. Not merely someone who can be convicted of being the killer. The actual man who did it. The whole discipline this book describes exists to make sure that the person delivered to a room full of grieving families is the right person, and in that room, I believed we had delivered the right person, because the evidence said so and the evidence was ours.

There was a billboard campaign during the investigation, with the faces of the victims on it, an appeal to the public for anything that might help. Those women were named on that billboard, and they deserve to be named as people rather than itemized as a body count. I did not know any of them, and I will not invent a familiarity I did not have. But they were the reason the room existed, and the reason the work mattered, and they are the reason I am telling the case in this order, from them forward, rather than from the offender backward.

One of the victims was a man, Thomas Steele. My read, and I mark it as my read, drawn from talking with the detectives and from the pattern the offender otherwise followed, is that Steele was most likely collateral rather than a chosen target of the kind Franklin pursued. I state that as opinion. The record does not establish it, and I will not pretend the record establishes it.

There was also a survivor. She lived through an attack that others did not survive, and her account was part of what the investigation was built on. Her name appeared in public reporting. I am not going to use it. By the same reasoning the prologue used, a person whose name became public through the worst thing that ever happened to her retains the right to control her own story, and this book will take nothing from her that she would not choose to give. That she survived is part of the record. The rest is hers.

Closure

Lonnie David Franklin Jr. died at San Quentin on March 28, 2020, before his death sentence was carried out. After he died, the cases that had been connected to him were closed. The families of victims who could be identified, by DNA or by the photographs recovered in the search, were told, informally, that the case was solved and closed. That is where the factual arc of the case ends.

I want to close on one thing, and it is the thing this whole chapter, and in a sense this whole book, has been trying to say.

The entire record of this case is public. Anyone can look it up. The dates, the victim names, the DNA, the trial, the sentence, all of it is a matter of record and available to anyone who wants to read it. And it becomes something entirely different when you are in the room with the families and the victims. That is the moment it stops being a case and becomes people. Everything in this book, all the methodology and the pillars and the linkage and the evidence, exists in service of that room. The discipline is not the point. The room is the point. The discipline is only how you earn the right to stand in it and tell the families that the person who did this has a name, and that the name is the right one.

ON THE RECORD

Established

- **The Grim Sleeper series ran across South Los Angeles from 1985 to 2007.** Lonnie David Franklin Jr. was convicted of ten counts of first-degree murder and one of attempted murder, and was sentenced to death on August 10, 2016. He died at San Quentin on March 28, 2020.
- **The name describes a detection gap, not a behavioral one.** The apparent fourteen-year hiatus reflected the disbanding of the task force in 1988 and the resulting failure to link cases, not any pause in the offender's activity. The investigators are on record that he never truly stopped.
- **Method changed; the evidence did not.** The early victims were shot, the later cluster included strangulations, and the two read as separate offenders until DNA and ballistics tied them to one hand. It is the signature-versus-method distinction from Chapter 4, inside a single case.
- **This was the first familial DNA search to identify a serial killer and lead to a murder conviction in the United States.** Not the first familial search in the country, but the first to catch a serial murderer and hold to a conviction. The technique was confirmed as no fluke when it caught Geovanni Borjas seven years later.

Myth

- **That the Grim Sleeper slept.** He did not. The gap was in the linkage, not in the killing, and treating the name as a description of the offender's behavior gets the entire case backward.
- **That a concealed room implies criminal genius.** In this case the concealment read as mimicry of serial-killer film tropes rather than sophistication. The hidden archive was informative not because it was clever but because it was kept.

- **That familial DNA and genetic genealogy are the same technique.** They are not. Franklin was caught by a law-enforcement database search for a convicted close relative. The later genetic-genealogy cases, including the Golden State Killer, used consumer ancestry databases and family-tree construction, which is a different method.

Still unsettled

- **The true victim count.** Ten are proven. More than forty are officially linked. My own recollection is of nearly twice the linked figure. The three numbers are three different kinds of claim, and I have kept them distinct.
- **Whether Thomas Steele was a chosen target.** My read, offered as opinion, is that the single male victim was most likely collateral rather than a victim of the type Franklin otherwise pursued. The record does not establish it.

Chapter 12: Killer Teams and the Pillars Under Partnership

Every case in this book so far has involved a single offender. The four pillars were built that way, for one person who hunts inside a comfort zone, who leaves a signature he cannot suppress, who keeps what he cannot bear to discard, and who selects victims he can reach without alarm. The framework works on solo offenders because solo offenders are what the standard literature was built to describe.

Team offenders are treated, in most of that literature, as a footnote. They should not be. Two people killing together are not a rare curiosity; they recur across the record, across countries, and across eras, and they raise a question the solo-offender framework cannot answer on its own. Do the pillars still hold when there are two hands instead of one? The honest answer is that they hold, that they change shape in the holding, and that the specific way each pillar changes is itself informative. This chapter is about that change, and about a single question that runs underneath all five of the cases in it: who was driving.

That question, who was driving, is the analytical spine of the chapter, because a team is not two identical offenders. In almost every documented partnership there is a dominant member and a compliant one, and the relationship between them shapes how every pillar reads. The comfort zone usually belongs to the dominant partner. The signature usually reflects the dominant partner's need. The victim-selection lure usually runs through the compliant partner. And the case, when it breaks, usually breaks through the compliant partner. So before the cases, the translation. Each pillar does something slightly different when a partnership is running the crime, and each difference points back at the structure of the partnership.

The comfort zone tends to belong to one partner rather than to both. The geography of a team's crimes usually tracks the dominant partner's world, and the compliant partner is frequently displaced into that world, brought into a zone that was not originally theirs. So a team's comfort zone is readable, but it is readable as one person's zone with a second person operating inside it, which is a different thing from two people sharing a zone equally. Identifying whose zone it is identifies the dominant partner.

The signature reflects the dominant partner's need, and it often runs more elaborate than a solo offender's signature would, because the compliant partner supplies logistics the dominant partner could not manage alone. One person can hold a victim while the other does something that requires both hands and uninterrupted time. Team signatures can therefore be more developed, more staged, and more documented than solo signatures, not because the dominant partner is more compulsive but because the partnership removes the practical limits that would otherwise constrain what a single offender can enact.

The trophies skew heavily toward documentation. This is the single most consistent finding across the recorded team cases, and it is worth stating plainly at the outset because the cases will keep returning to it. A solo offender who wants to relive a crime has to rely on memory or on a physical object taken from the scene. A team can record. A second person makes photography, audio, and video practical in a way they are not for a lone offender occupied with the crime itself. And the recordings, once made, are the most self-incriminating category of evidence in the entire record, because they document the crime directly rather than merely connecting an offender to it. The trophy a team keeps is frequently the exact thing that convicts the team.

Victim selection gains a mechanism solo offenders lack. A lone male offender approaching a potential victim generates a specific kind of alarm. A man and a woman together, or a woman alone making the initial approach, generate far less. The compliant partner, very often the female member of a male-female team, functions as a disarming presence, a lure that extends access to victims a solo male offender could not approach. This does not change the demographics of who is selected. It changes who can be reached, and it widens the reachable population considerably.

Method shifts because two people can do what one cannot. The capability-and-access calculus from Chapter 5 changes when there are two sets of hands. Restraint becomes easier, transport becomes easier, a victim can be controlled by one partner while the other drives or keeps watch or prepares. Methods that would be impractical for a solo offender become available to a team, which means method choice in a team case reveals the partnership as much as it reveals either individual.

Those are the five translations. The cases that follow illustrate them, and each leans hardest on one or two while all are present to some degree. I have chosen five, deliberately spanning different partnership structures, different eras, and different countries, because the point of the chapter is that the pattern is general and not an artifact of one time or place. In each, the first question I ask is the one that organizes everything else. Who was driving.

Gerald and Charlene Gallego

Gerald Gallego and Charlene Williams operated across California, Nevada, and Oregon between 1978 and 1980, and are confirmed responsible for ten murders. For a reader coming to the case fresh, the essential facts are these. Gerald Gallego was a Sacramento man with a long criminal history and, by the accounts that emerged at trial, a fixation on the idea of keeping captive victims he called sex slaves. Charlene Williams was a younger woman from a comfortable background who became his wife, using an assumed name for part of the period. Over roughly two years the pair abducted, held, sexually assaulted, and killed ten people, most of them teenagers and young adults taken in pairs, across three states. They were caught in 1980 after their final abduction, of a young couple in Sacramento, was partly witnessed. Charlene ultimately cooperated with the prosecution, and Gerald was sentenced to death.

The question of who was driving has, in this case, an unusually clean answer, and the answer organizes every pillar. Gerald drove. Charlene, ten years younger, was the compliant partner, and the case is the clearest illustration in the American record of what a compliant partner makes possible, because the partnership's entire method depended on her in a way that was structural rather than incidental.

The dominance in the relationship is established by more than testimony, though the testimony is consistent. It is established by the shape of the crimes themselves. The fantasy being enacted was Gerald's; the concept of a captive victim was his; the escalation across the two years was his. Charlene's role was defined by that fantasy and subordinate to it. This matters methodologically because it tells the investigator where to locate the signature. The signature in a team case belongs to the person whose need is being served, and in the Gallego case the need being served was unambiguously Gerald's. Charlene enabled it. She did not originate it.

The comfort zone was Gerald's, and Charlene was displaced into it. Sacramento was his territory, the region he knew and moved through without friction, and the geography of the killings tracks his world rather than hers. This is the dominant-partner geography the framing section described, and it is worth noticing how reliably it holds. An investigator who can identify whose comfort zone a team is operating in has very often identified the dominant partner, because the compliant partner is the one who was brought into a world not originally theirs.

Victim selection is where this case earns its place in the chapter, because the lure mechanism ran as a formal procedure rather than an occasional tactic. The pattern was consistent enough to be described as a method. Charlene, a small and unthreatening young woman, would approach victims, frequently teenagers, in public places such as shopping malls and fairgrounds. A young woman approaching other young people is not a threat and generates no alarm, and that absence of alarm was the entire point. Once the victims were drawn in, Gerald took over.

Read against Chapter 4, the mechanism is precise. The demographics of the victims follow the ordinary logic of availability and vulnerability, the same logic that governs solo cases. What the partnership changed was access. The lure did not alter who was desirable to the offender; it altered who was reachable. A lone man attempting the same approaches would have generated alarm at the first contact and been remembered, described, and avoided. Charlene generated none, because a young woman is not what a potential victim has been taught to fear. She was the access multiplier, and she multiplied Gerald's reach to include victims he could never have approached alone. That is the victim-selection pillar with a second person attached, and the second person is the compliant partner.

The method, too, shows the partnership. The victims were abducted and held, which is a two-person method. A solo offender abducting a victim must simultaneously control, transport, and conceal, which is difficult and dangerous and self-limiting. A team divides those tasks. One controls while the other drives. The capability the partnership provided was not skill; it was hands, and the additional hands made a category of crime practical that would have been impractical for either of them alone.

The case ended in 1980, and it ended the way team cases characteristically end, through the compliant partner. Charlene took a plea agreement, testified against Gerald, and was sentenced to sixteen years; she was paroled in 1997. Gerald was sentenced to death and died in prison in 2002. The plea-and-testify resolution is not incidental to the partnership structure. It is a consequence of it. The compliant partner knows everything the dominant partner did, because she was present for all of it, and once the partnership is broken and she is separated from the dominant partner's influence, she has both the knowledge and the incentive to testify. The dominant partner's control, which held the partnership together while it operated, becomes the prosecution's single greatest asset the moment the partnership fractures. The synthesis will return to this, because it recurs in nearly every case in the chapter.

Doug Clark and Carol Bundy

Doug Clark and Carol Bundy killed in Los Angeles in the summer of 1980, in and around the Sunset Strip, which gave the case its popular name. Clark was convicted of six first-degree murders, an attempted murder, and mutilation of human remains, and was sentenced to death in 1983; he died on death row in 2023. Bundy was convicted of two murders, was sentenced to fifty-two years to life, and died in prison in 2003. This is the case where the question of who was driving does not have a clean answer, and that is exactly why it belongs in the chapter, because it shows where the dominant-and-compliant model has to be applied with care rather than mechanically.

The basic shape of the case, for a reader meeting it for the first time, is this. Doug Clark and Carol Bundy met in a North Hollywood bar around Christmas of 1979. Clark was a factory worker who habitually seduced older women for money and lodging; Bundy was a divorced vocational nurse with a history of abuse and instability. They moved in together quickly. Over the summer of 1980 they killed at least six women and girls, most of them runaways and sex workers, in and around the Sunset Strip in Los Angeles. Clark shot most of the victims and committed sexual acts on the bodies. The spree ended in August 1980 when Bundy, having separately killed a former lover she feared could expose them, broke down and confessed to her co-workers, who called the police. Clark was convicted and sentenced to death and died in prison in 2023; Bundy pleaded to two murders and died in prison in 2003.

The popular version of the relationship is simple. Clark was the dominant partner, a practiced manipulator who worked bars for lonely women he could use for money and housing, and Bundy was the vulnerable, love-starved nurse he drew into his crimes. There is real truth in that version. Clark did target Bundy as, in the words of one person who interviewed both of them, easy prey. He did introduce the murders. The comfort zone was his, the Sunset Strip corridor he worked, and the victims were the runaways and sex workers available there, which is Chapter 4's victim selection running in its ordinary channel.

But the people who actually spent time with both offenders came away with a more complicated picture, and the complication is instructive for anyone applying this framework. Journalists who interviewed Bundy described her as colder, darker, and in some respects cleverer than the passive-victim story allows. She was not merely present. She killed a man on her own, a former lover named Jack Murray, without Clark, because she believed Murray knew too much. And the physical evidence resists the clean binary in a way worth dwelling on, because physical evidence is what this book trusts over narrative. The pistol used in the shootings was registered to Carol Bundy, not to Clark. The trophies recovered from the case, including items taken from victims and a photographic record of an assault, were in Bundy's keeping and were handed over by her. The compliant partner, in other words, was the registered owner of the murder weapon and the keeper of the documentation.

What that complication teaches is that the dominant-and-compliant model is a lens, not a law. It describes a real and recurring structure, and in most cases it maps cleanly, as it did with the Gallegos. But a team is two people, and two people are capable of a relationship more tangled than a simple hierarchy. In the Clark and Bundy case, the most defensible reading of the evidence is that Clark was the originating and dominant force, the one whose fantasy set the direction, but that Bundy was a fully active participant whose own capacity for violence was real and independent, not merely borrowed from him. The methodological instruction is to hold the model loosely enough to see this. An investigator who assumes the female partner in a male-female team is necessarily passive will misread the evidence, and in this case would have misread the registration of the weapon and the custody of the trophies.

The signature in the case was Clark's, expressed through acts the partnership made possible, and it took a form severe enough that I will describe it at the level the methodology requires and no further. Clark kept parts of victims. The keeping is the trophy principle from Chapter 4, and the partnership is what made it practical, because a second person removes the logistical limits on what an offender occupied with the crime can manage. The documentation pattern, the chapter's recurring finding, appears here in the kept trophies and the photographic record rather than in audio or video, but it appears, and it appears in the compliant partner's custody, which is the detail that broke the case.

Because the case broke, as these cases do, through the second partner. Bundy killed Murray, and afterward broke down and confessed to her co-workers at the medical center where she worked. Those co-workers called the police. When the police arrived, Bundy handed over the trophies she had kept. The partnership's collapse came from within, through the compliant partner, exactly as it did with the Gallegos, and the trophies she surrendered were a substantial part of the evidence against Clark. The keeper of the documentation became the source of the documentation's delivery to the prosecution, which is the team-trophy pattern folding directly into the compliant-partner-fracture pattern. Both of the chapter's structural findings are present in the single act of Carol Bundy handing evidence to a police officer.

Lawrence Bittaker and Roy Norris

Lawrence Bittaker and Roy Norris met in prison and, after their respective releases, killed five teenage girls in Southern California in 1979. The case is the purest illustration in the American record of the documentation-becomes-evidence pattern, and it is the case that most clearly demonstrates why the trophy a team keeps is so often the thing that convicts it. On the question of who was driving, the record supports a reading of Bittaker as the dominant partner and Norris as the follower, but this case complicates the compliant-partner model in the opposite direction from the Clark and Bundy case, because here the compliant partner was not a manipulated vulnerable person but a fellow convict with his own history of sexual violence.

The essential facts, for a reader who does not know the case, are these, and they are difficult ones. Between June 24 and October 31 of 1979, Bittaker and Norris abducted, assaulted, tortured, and murdered five girls in Los Angeles County: Lucinda Schaefer, sixteen; Andrea Hall, eighteen; Jacqueline Gilliam, fifteen; Leah Lamp, thirteen; and Shirley Ledford, sixteen. They used a van they had modified for the purpose, and they took their victims to remote fire roads in the San Gabriel Mountains. Two of the victims' bodies were never recovered. The case broke in late 1979 when Norris talked about the crimes to a former prison acquaintance, who told police, and when a woman who had survived an earlier assault by the pair was able to identify them. Norris confessed and agreed to testify against Bittaker in exchange for a sentence of forty-five years to life. Bittaker was convicted on all counts and sentenced to death.

The partnership originated in prison, where the two men met and, according to the trial record, discussed their shared interest in the abduction and rape of women, analyzing methods of doing it without being caught. This is worth pausing on, because it distinguishes the case from the Gallego and Clark cases. The partnership was not one offender drawing a vulnerable person into his world. It was two offenders finding each other and combining. The dominance that emerged, Bittaker's, was a dominance within a partnership of two willing participants, which is a different structure from a dominant partner and a captive one, and it shows that the compliant-partner model has more than one form.

The comfort zone was a constructed and mobile one. The two men equipped a van for the purpose of the crimes, and used it to abduct victims from Southern California roadways. The van was the anchor, a mobile venue engineered for the crime, and it made the partnership's method possible. This is the comfort zone as a physical construction rather than a geographic area, a thread this book has followed from the discussion of purpose-built venues, and it is a thread the next chapter will pick up in a historical case. The van was to Bittaker and Norris what a fixed structure was to other offenders, an environment they controlled completely, and the control the environment provided is part of what enabled the severity of what happened inside it.

The method shows the two-sets-of-hands advantage in its most literal form. The partnership enabled a division of labor in which one man drove and kept watch while the other committed the assault, communicating by radio. A solo offender cannot simultaneously abduct, transport, control, and assault; the tasks conflict. A team resolves the conflict by dividing the tasks, and the division is what made the crimes practical. The method, read as evidence, points directly at the partnership, because no solo offender could have done what the physical arrangement of the crimes required.

The documentation is the center of the case and the reason it anchors the chapter. The pair recorded audio of the torture and murder of their final victim, a sixteen-year-old girl, and Bittaker also took photographs of victims, some of which entered the trial record. The audio recording ran roughly seventeen minutes. Here is the point the entire chapter is building toward, stated in its single clearest instance. The recording was not merely a trophy the offenders kept to relive the crime, though it was that. It was the prosecution's evidence. When Norris was arrested first and Bittaker had a brief window to destroy evidence, he missed the tape, and the tape was found in his van. Played at trial, it was reportedly a significant factor in the jury's decision to return a death sentence, and jurors are on record describing the effect it had on them, some reporting lasting distress. The thing the team made in order to relive the crime became the thing that proved the crime beyond any argument the defense could offer.

That is the documentation pattern at its most extreme, and it is why the framing section flagged documentation as the most consistent and most consequential of the team-specific findings. A solo offender who keeps a physical trophy gives the prosecution an object that must still be connected to a crime through other evidence. A team that records the crime gives the prosecution the crime itself, in the offenders' own voices. The recording collapses the distance between trophy and proof. It is simultaneously the most private thing the offenders possessed and the most public thing the trial produced.

The case resolved through the compliant partner, the pattern holding for the third time. Norris pleaded guilty, testified against Bittaker, and received a sentence of forty-five years to life. Bittaker was sentenced to death. The follower testified against the driver, the partnership fractured along the line of dominance, and the compliant partner's cooperation was decisive. Even in a partnership of two willing offenders rather than a dominant-and-captive pair, the fracture ran the same direction, from the follower toward the leader, because the follower had less to lose and the prosecution had more to offer him.

Leonard Lake and Charles Ng

Leonard Lake and Charles Ng operated in California in the early to mid-1980s, primarily from a rural property Lake controlled in Calaveras County. The case combines two of the chapter's threads, the documentation pattern and a constructed anchor point in the lineage of the purpose-built venue, and it is among the most severe in the record by victim count, though the exact number remains uncertain. On the question of who was driving, the record is genuinely contested, and the contest is itself instructive, because it became the central question of Ng's trial.

The case in brief, for a reader new to it, runs as follows. Leonard Lake was a survivalist who controlled a remote property in Calaveras County, in the Sierra foothills, where he had built a fortified structure including a concrete bunker. Charles Ng was a younger man Lake had met some years earlier. Operating from the property in the mid-1980s, the pair lured, held, and killed a number of victims, including at least one entire family, and documented much of what they did. The operation came apart in June 1985 almost by accident, when Ng was caught shoplifting at a store in South San Francisco and Lake, who was with him, was detained. Lake took a concealed cyanide capsule and died days later. Ng fled to Canada, was arrested there, and after years of extradition litigation was returned to California, tried, and convicted of eleven murders. It is one of the most severe cases in the American record, and the true victim count is higher than the convictions but has never been precisely established.

Lake was the older partner, the property owner, the keeper of the written records, and by most readings the originating force. Ng was younger, and his defense at trial argued that Lake was the sole offender and that Ng was a follower whose participation was more limited than the prosecution alleged. The jury did not fully accept that argument, convicting Ng of eleven murders, but it did acquit him on some counts, which means the exact division of responsibility between the two men was never established to the certainty that the Gallego or Bittaker cases reached. This is worth stating honestly, because the dominant-and-compliant model is a lens for reading evidence, not a substitute for it, and in this case the evidence left the precise structure of the partnership partly unresolved. What is clear is that Lake controlled the anchor and originated the documentation, which points at Lake as the dominant partner, but the degree of Ng's subordination remained a live question.

The anchor point in this case was a physical construction, and it is the purest example in the chapter of the comfort zone as engineered venue rather than familiar geography. Lake's property included a bunker built for the purpose of holding victims. This places it in the same category as the purpose-built venue this book discusses in the historical context, the anchor that is not merely a familiar area but a structure designed for the crime. The partnership made the construction and operation of such a venue practical in a way it would not have been for a solo offender. Building, concealing, provisioning, and operating a dedicated structure is a substantial undertaking, and the second set of hands is part of what made it feasible. The team advantage, in this case, applied to the anchor-point pillar itself, not merely to method or selection. Two people can build and run a venue that one person could not.

The documentation pattern appears here in its fullest form, across multiple media, and it is central to how the case is understood. Lake kept a written record, a diary that documented aspects of the operation, and the pair recorded video of victims. The written and recorded material, taken together, documented the nature and scale of the crimes in a way that testimony alone could not have, and as in the Bittaker and Norris case, the material the team made for its own purposes became the evidence that established what had happened. The documentation pattern and the dominant-partner question intersect here, because Lake was the documentarian, and the fact that he was the one keeping the records is itself evidence about who was driving. The person who compulsively documents a partnership's crimes is very often the person whose need the crimes are serving.

The case broke in 1985 through an almost incidental event that had nothing to do with the investigation of the murders, which is a recurring and humbling feature of these cases. Ng was caught shoplifting. Lake, present, was taken into custody, and shortly afterward died by suicide using a concealed cyanide capsule. Ng fled the country, was eventually located and extradited after a lengthy international legal process, and was ultimately convicted of eleven murders. Here the compliant-partner-fracture pattern takes a different form than in the earlier cases, because the dominant partner died before trial rather than the compliant partner testifying against him. But the underlying structure is visible even in the variation. The partnership ended, and once it ended, the surviving partner faced the full weight of the documentation the dominant partner had created. Lake's records and recordings, made to serve the partnership, convicted the man who survived it. The documentation outlived the documentarian and did the prosecution's work after his death.

The victim count is genuinely uncertain, and estimates run considerably higher than the eleven convictions. In keeping with the discipline this book has maintained from the prologue forward, I state the eleven as the proven figure and mark the higher estimates as unproven. The gap between the two numbers is itself a version of the undercount problem from the Samuel Little chapter, and it is wider in this case than in most, because the destruction and concealment at the site made a full accounting impossible.

The Gonzalez Sisters

The final case is deliberately the furthest from the others, in country, in era, and in partnership structure, because the point of including it is to show that the team pattern is not an artifact of a particular time or place. Delfina and Maria de Jesus Gonzalez, with the involvement of two other sisters, ran a prostitution operation in the Mexican states of Guanajuato and Jalisco from roughly 1950 until 1964. They were known, after the fact, as Las Poquianchis. They were tried in 1964 and each principal sentenced to forty years, the maximum under Mexican law at the time.

For a reader unfamiliar with the case, which is far less known in the United States than the American cases in this chapter, the essential facts are these. The sisters ran a network of brothels centered on a ranch. They obtained young women by deception, holding them in conditions of captivity and forced prostitution. Women who became ill, or aged out of the operation's purposes, or resisted, were killed and buried on the property, as were some of their children and some male customers who were robbed. The operation ran for well over a decade before it was exposed in early 1964, when a young woman escaped and went to the authorities, leading to a search of the property that uncovered the graves. The scale of what was found made the case a national trauma in Mexico and gave the sisters a permanent place in the country's criminal history.

On the question of who was driving, this case answers differently from the others, and the difference is the reason it belongs. This is not a dominant-and-compliant dyad. It is a family business, run by sisters, with Delfina generally identified as the matriarchal head and the others operating within a shared enterprise rather than under a single dominant partner's control. The relevant structure is not a hierarchy of two but a family organization, and that difference matters for the framework, because it shows that the pillars translate even when the partnership is not the dominant-and-compliant pair the American cases in this chapter kept producing. The comfort zone, the victim selection, the method, all still read, but they read through a family enterprise rather than a couple. The framework is not describing a specific relationship type. It is describing what happens when more than one person shares the work, and the sharing can take the form of a couple or a family or a business, or, in this case, all three at once.

The comfort zone was the ranch, a controlled property that functioned as both anchor and venue, in the same category as the Lake bunker and the historical purpose-built venues, though at far larger scale. The property was the operation's fixed point, the place the enterprise was run from and the place the killings occurred, and it was the sisters' shared territory in the way a dominant partner's geography was the Gallegos' shared zone. A controlled property operated by a family is a comfort zone by any definition this book has used, and the fact that it was operated by four people rather than one is precisely what allowed it to run at the scale it did.

Victim selection is where the case demonstrates something no other case in the chapter can, because it ran the lure mechanism at industrial scale. The Gallego case showed the lure operating at the scale of individual encounters, one compliant partner approaching one victim at a time. The Gonzalez operation formalized the same mechanism into a business process. They recruited young women through help-wanted advertisements offering domestic work. The advertisement is the lure abstracted from any individual and turned into a standing procedure, a disarming approach that operated continuously and at volume. Women answered advertisements for maid positions and were trafficked into the operation, and when they became ill, or ceased to be profitable, or otherwise stopped serving the enterprise, they were killed. Customers were sometimes killed and robbed as well. The access mechanism the framing section described, the disarming approach that extends reach to victims a direct approach could not obtain, ran here as an advertising campaign. That is the victim-selection pillar scaled from a tactic to an institution, and only a multi-person enterprise could have operated it.

When the property was searched, authorities recovered the remains of at least ninety-one people, comprising by the contemporary accounting roughly eighty women, eleven men, and fetal remains. Estimates of the true total run considerably higher, to a hundred and fifty or beyond, and Guinness World Records has described the sisters as the most prolific murder partnership on record. I state the ninety-one as the recovered figure and mark the higher numbers as estimates, which is the same three-tier honesty this book has applied to every contested count from the prologue forward.

The Gonzalez case tests the framework at its outer edge, and the framework holds. The comfort zone was a controlled property functioning as anchor and venue. Victim selection ran through a lure mechanism operated by the enterprise at industrial scale. And the undercount problem from the Samuel Little chapter appears here in its international and historical form, because a trafficking operation killing marginalized women in rural Mexico across the 1950s is precisely the kind of series the detection apparatus of its time and place was least equipped to see. It ran for well over a decade before an escaped victim brought it down, not because it was hidden with any particular sophistication, but because the victims were exactly the people whose disappearances generated no official concern. The pillars translate across the border and across the decades, and the specific institutional context changes what each pillar looks like without changing the logic underneath. That was the claim the framing section made, and the Gonzalez case is the strongest single test of it in the book, because it is the case that shares the least with the framework's origins and conforms to it anyway.

What the Teams Teach

Five cases, three partnership structures, two countries, and one consistent result. The pillars hold. They change shape under partnership, and the changes are the lesson. Running underneath all of them is the question the chapter opened with, who was driving, and in four of the five cases the answer was clear enough to organize everything else. In the fifth, Clark and Bundy, the answer was genuinely tangled, and the tangle was its own lesson.

The comfort zone belongs to the dominant partner, and the compliant partner is displaced into it. This held for the Gallegos, for Clark and Bundy, and, through the constructed venue, for Bittaker and Norris and for Lake and Ng, and it held in the family form for the Gonzalez enterprise. Reading a team's geography means reading whose geography it is, because the answer points at the dominant partner and, through the dominant partner, at the structure of the partnership itself. When the zone is a constructed venue rather than a familiar area, the person who built and controlled it is very often the person who was driving.

The signature reflects the dominant partner's need and runs more elaborate than a solo signature would, because the second partner supplies the logistics that a lone offender lacks. The staging a partnership makes possible is visible across the cases, and it is why team crimes can appear, on the surface, more organized and more deliberate than the crimes of a solo offender of comparable compulsion. The organization is not greater compulsion. It is the removal of the practical limits a single pair of hands imposes. The person whose need the staging serves is the dominant partner, and identifying the signature identifies him.

The trophies skew toward documentation, and the documentation convicts. This is the finding that recurs most forcefully across the cases, from the

Bittaker and Norris audiotape to the Lake and Ng video and diary to the trophies in Carol Bundy's keeping. A second person makes recording practical, and a recording is the most self-incriminating evidence in the record, because it is the crime itself rather than a link to it. The team keeps the thing that convicts the team. And the keeper of the documentation is frequently a clue to who was driving, because the person who compulsively records the partnership's crimes is very often the person whose need the crimes serve. If there is a single practical lesson in this chapter for an investigator working a suspected team case, it is that the documentation almost certainly exists, that finding it is very often the whole case, and that identifying who kept it points at the dominant partner.

Victim selection gains the lure, and the lure widens access. The demographics do not change; the reachable population does. The Gallego procedure and the Gonzalez help-wanted advertisements are the same mechanism at two different scales, the disarming approach that extends the partnership's reach to victims a solo offender could not have approached, and the lure very often runs through the compliant partner, which is another place the partnership structure becomes visible in the evidence. This is Chapter 4's victim-selection pillar with an access multiplier attached, and the multiplier is the second partner.

And there is the recurring endgame, which nearly every case in this chapter shared and which is worth naming as its own finding. The partnership breaks through the compliant partner. Charlene Gallego testified against Gerald. Carol Bundy confessed and broke the case and handed over the trophies. Roy Norris pleaded and testified against Bittaker. In the Lake and Ng case the pattern varied, because the dominant partner died before trial, but even there the structure held, because the documentation the dominant partner created convicted the partner who survived him. The dominant partner's control, which held while the partnership was intact, becomes the prosecution's advantage the moment the partnership fractures, because the compliant partner knows everything and, once separated from the dominant partner's influence, has both the knowledge and every incentive to tell it. A solo offender has no one who can turn on him. A team is, by its nature, one fracture away from a confession. That is not a pillar. It is a structural vulnerability specific to partnership, and it is the reason team cases, for all the access and capability the second partner provides, so often end with one member testifying against the other.

The pillars were built for one offender. They survive the addition of a second, and reading them under partnership means reading the partnership itself, its dominant member, its compliant member, its documentation, and the fracture that so often ends it. The framework does not break when a second hand enters the crime. It gains a dimension, and the dimension is the relationship between the two people committing it. The first question, always, is who was driving, and every pillar, read carefully, helps answer it.

ON THE RECORD

Established

- **The four pillars translate to team offenders.** Comfort zone, signature, trophies, and victim selection all appear in team cases, each modified by the presence of a second offender in a specific and readable way that points back at the structure of the partnership.
- **A team's comfort zone usually belongs to the dominant partner.** The compliant partner is displaced into the dominant partner's geography, and when the zone is a constructed venue rather than a familiar area, the person who built and controlled it is very often the one who was driving.
- **Team trophies skew toward documentation, and the documentation convicts.** Audio, video, photographs, and written records are practical for a team in a way they are not for a solo offender, and the recording is the most self-incriminating evidence in the record because it is the crime itself. Bittaker and Norris, and Lake and Ng, are the paradigm cases.
- **The lure widens access without changing demographics.** A disarming approach, very often by the compliant partner, extends the team's reach to victims a solo offender could not approach. The Gallego procedure and the Gonzalez help-wanted advertisements are the same mechanism at different scales.

- **Team cases frequently break through the compliant partner.** Once the partnership fractures, the compliant partner knows everything and has every incentive to testify. Charlene Gallego, Carol Bundy, and Roy Norris each turned on the dominant partner; in the Lake and Ng case the dominant partner's own documentation did the equivalent work after his death.

Myth

- **That the female partner in a male-female team is necessarily passive.** The Clark and Bundy case shows the danger of that assumption; the murder weapon was registered to the compliant partner, and she was the keeper of the trophies and committed a murder independently. The dominant-and-compliant model is a lens, not a law.
- **That team crimes reflect greater compulsion or organization than solo crimes.** The apparent organization comes from the removal of the practical limits a single offender faces, not from a greater underlying drive. The second partner supplies logistics, not compulsion.
- **That team offenders are a rare curiosity outside the main pattern.** They recur across the record, across countries, and across eras, and the standard literature's treatment of them as a footnote understates how consistently the pattern appears.

Still unsettled

- **The true victim counts in several of these cases.** Lake and Ng, and the Gonzalez operation in particular, carry proven figures well below the estimated ones. The convictions are firm; the totals are not.
- **The exact division of responsibility in contested partnerships.** The Lake and Ng case never fully resolved how the work was divided between the two men, and the Clark and Bundy relationship may never be fully understood. The framework locates the dominant partner; it does not always settle the precise share of each partner's hand.

Chapter 13: The Venue and the Legend

In the summer of 1895, a Philadelphia detective named Frank Geyer was digging in the cellar of a rented house in Toronto. He had been traveling for weeks, across several states and into Canada, following a trail that most of his colleagues thought led nowhere. He was looking for three children. He found two of them in that cellar.

Geyer had no crime laboratory. There would not be one in the United States for another twenty-eight years. He had no fingerprint database, no forensic pathology in any modern sense, no way to test a fiber or a stain that we would recognize today. What he had was a bundle of letters. The children had written them to their mother and to relatives during the months they were being moved from city to city, and the man who had taken them had never mailed them. He had kept them instead. When that man was arrested, the letters were found among his possessions, and Geyer read them, and the letters named the cities. The children had written down, without knowing it, the route of their own disappearance. Geyer followed the route until it ended in two cellars and an Indiana rental, and the trail closed.

The man who had taken them was named Herman Webster Mudgett, though the world would come to know him by a name he invented, Dr. H.H. Holmes, and by a legend that has almost nothing to do with what Frank Geyer actually found. That gap, between the legend and the record, is the subject of this chapter.

Why a Forensic Book Opens Its History Before the Crime Lab

A reasonable objection presents itself at the start of any historical chapter in a book about forensic methodology. If the book is about how forensic evidence catches serial killers, why reach back to the eighteen-nineties and the nineteen-hundreds, to cases that predate the crime laboratory entirely? There was no lab. There was no standardized fingerprinting in American practice, no forensic serology, none of the apparatus the word forensics now calls to mind. What can cases from before the science teach a book about the science?

The objection rests on the same misconception this entire book exists to correct, which is the belief that forensics means the crime lab and the crime lab means forensics. It does not. Forensics is a wide federation of disciplines, and the image most people carry, the bench with the microscope and the DNA sequencer, is one sliver of it. The family includes financial and questioned-document examination, forensic photography, digital and multimedia evidence, odontology, toxicology, forensic anthropology, pattern and impression evidence, and a good deal more. Some of these disciplines are more than a century old. Some of them are older than the laboratory that later gave them a shared roof.

The acknowledged institutional history of American forensic science begins with a specific date and place. The first crime laboratory in the United States was established by the Los Angeles Police Department in July of 1923, under Chief August Vollmer. Vollmer's Scientific Investigation Division would grow over the following decades to include units for questioned documents and for forensic photography, among others. The first crime laboratory in the world had opened thirteen years earlier, in 1910, when Edmond Locard founded his laboratory in Lyon, France. That is where the lab, as an institution, begins. It is not where forensic work begins.

I have a personal stake in this distinction, so I will state it once and move on. My own career was spent at the Los Angeles Police Department, in the division whose lineage runs directly back to Vollmer's, and my own discipline, forensic photography, is one of the non-laboratory forensic disciplines, a member of the wide federation rather than the narrow one. I know from twenty years inside it that the forensic family is broader than the lab bench, because I spent my career in one of the rooms that is not the lab. So when I say that Holmes and Gunness were caught by forensic work, I am not stretching the word. I am using it correctly.

Holmes predates the American crime lab by nearly three decades, and he was caught anyway, by the direct ancestors of financial and documentary forensics. The insurance policy. The aliases. The money trail. The kept letters. And a detective who did missing-person legwork across a continent.

The techniques that caught him existed a full generation before the labels and the laboratory did. That is the first thing this chapter is here to show, and Holmes shows it better than any case in the modern record could, precisely because there was no lab to share the credit.

The Man Behind the Legend

Herman Webster Mudgett was born in 1861 in Gilmanton, New Hampshire. He trained in medicine, which in his era and his hands meant primarily that he understood insurance, anatomy, and the paperwork of death well enough to defraud all three. He took the name Dr. H.H. Holmes, and he built a career out of confidence schemes. This is the essential fact about him, and the legend works hard to obscure it. Holmes was, before and beneath everything else, a financial criminal. He murdered to collect on policies, to cover earlier frauds, and to clear people out of the way of a scheme. The money is not a footnote to the killing. The money is the reason for the killing, and keeping the frame on the money is what makes the rest of the case legible, because the money is also what caught him.

The popular picture is entirely different, and it is worth naming its most influential modern source directly, because most readers who think they know Holmes know him through it. Erik Larson's The Devil in the White City, published in 2003, told the story of Holmes against the backdrop of the 1893 World's Columbian Exposition in Chicago, and told it well enough to fix a particular image of Holmes in the public mind for a generation. That image is of a purpose-built murder hotel, a castle in the Englewood neighborhood engineered from the ground up for killing, luring World's Fair visitors into trapdoors and soundproofed chambers and chutes that fed a basement dissection room and crematorium, where Holmes murdered as many as two hundred strangers.

Larson's book is careful narrative history, not pulp, and it drew on the sources available to it, which included the inflated contemporary accounts of the eighteen-nineties. The archival work that has since gone back to the primary records tells a different story. The most thorough of that work is Adam Selzer's 2017 history, H.H. Holmes: The True History of the White City Devil, which went to the deeds, the court records, the newspapers, and the physical history of the building itself. What Selzer establishes is that the murder castle, as a machine built to kill strangers, is largely a myth.

The Castle That Was Not a Castle

The building was real. It stood in Englewood, and Holmes owned and controlled it, and it was genuinely strange in its construction. But it was not a functioning hotel, and it was not built to kill. The ground floor held storefronts, ordinary retail space. The second floor held apartments, occupied by long-term tenants. The third floor, the part the legend turns into a hotel of horrors, was never finished, never furnished, and never opened to guests. It existed mainly as a vehicle for fraud, a way to swindle the suppliers, investors, and insurers who put money and materials into a hotel that was never going to operate.

The building did have odd features. There were hidden spaces and a vault built nearly soundproof, and the legend has made a great deal of them. The evidence, as Selzer reads it, points somewhere far more ordinary and far more consistent with who Holmes actually was. The concealed rooms and the dumbwaiters and the strange internal architecture were, in the main, ways to hide furniture and goods that Holmes had bought on credit and did not intend to pay for, keeping them out of sight of the repossession agents who came looking. The hidden spaces of the murder castle were, on the evidence, hiding places for unpaid-for furniture. There is no evidence of victims gassed in airtight rooms, and no evidence of a basement dissection laboratory. The machinery of the murder castle is, in its lurid particulars, a newspaper invention.

I am not going to walk through the invented architecture piece by piece, because reproducing the legend in detail, even to knock it down, is its own kind of dishonesty; it leaves the images in the reader's mind after the correction is forgotten. It is enough to say that the specific apparatus the legend sells was not there, and to note why the correction matters for this book. This chapter opens the historical head of a lineage that ran through Chapter 12: the purpose-built venue, the space engineered for the crime, the Bittaker van and the Lake bunker and the Gonzalez ranch. Holmes is the most famous purpose-built murder venue in the popular imagination. And the honest version of Holmes is that his venue was substantially a legend. The man controlled a building and used it in his frauds. He did not build a machine for killing strangers. That is the more interesting truth, and it is the one the record supports.

It matters for a second reason, which reaches to the heart of who Holmes actually killed. The people Holmes can be shown, with reasonable confidence, to have murdered were not strangers pulled off the fairgrounds and fed into a machine. They were people he knew. Associates, business partners, women he had romanced, people entangled in his financial schemes. He killed the people whose deaths paid, or whose deaths covered, or whose continued existence threatened a fraud. The killing did not depend on the building the way the legend insists it did. It depended on the relationship, and the relationship is what put the victim within reach. This is Chapter 4's victim-selection principle wearing period dress. Holmes selected victims he had access to, and his access came through acquaintance and business and courtship, not through a trapdoor.

The Scheme That Ended Him

The case that hanged Holmes had nothing to do with the castle. It was an insurance fraud, and it is the clearest illustration in the historical record of financial forensics doing the work a crime lab would later be credited with.

Holmes and a longtime associate named Benjamin Pitezel arranged a life-insurance fraud built on a ten-thousand-dollar policy on Pitezel's life. The plan, as Pitezel understood it, was to fake his death, substitute a cadaver, and split the payout. Holmes improved on the plan from his own point of view by dispensing with the cadaver and simply killing Pitezel, in Philadelphia in 1894, where Pitezel had been living under the alias B.F. Perry. A faked death is cheaper and safer to arrange when it is a real one, and Holmes was a man who followed that logic wherever it led.

The scheme unraveled through a loose thread Holmes had left behind him. Earlier, while jailed in St. Louis on a separate swindle, Holmes had described the insurance plan to a cellmate, an outlaw named Marion Hedgepeth, and had promised Hedgepeth a fee, commonly reported as five hundred dollars, for referring a lawyer who could help execute it. Holmes did not pay. Hedgepeth, unpaid and imprisoned and therefore possessed of both a grievance and time, informed on him. The tip put investigators onto the scheme, and the insurer, Fidelity Mutual, already uneasy about the claim, pressed harder. With Pinkerton involvement, the investigation closed in, and Holmes was arrested in Boston on the seventeenth of November, 1894, initially on the fraud.

Consider what did the work in that sequence, because none of it is what a modern reader means by forensics and all of it is forensics. An insurer's suspicion about a claim, which is the ancestor of the entire field of insurance and financial-fraud investigation. A money trail with an unpaid debt at the end of it, which is the work that would later be named forensic accounting and financial forensics, practiced here decades before it had a name. A set of aliases penetrated. A tip run down. No one in 1894 held the title of forensic accountant, and I am not suggesting anyone did. The point is the reverse. The discipline is older than its label. The work that caught Holmes was financial-forensic work in everything but name, performed a generation before there was a laboratory to house it or a job title to describe it.

The Children, and the Letters

The fraud arrest is what put Holmes in custody. It is not what revealed the murders. That was Frank Geyer, and the three Pitezel children, and it is the human center of the case.

After Benjamin Pitezel was dead, Holmes took three of the Pitezel children, telling their mother, Carrie, that their father was alive and in hiding and that the children needed to be brought to him. Carrie did not know she was a widow. She was manipulated into letting Holmes travel with her children across the country, believing she was being reunited with her husband by degrees. The children were Alice, who was fifteen, Nellie, who was eleven, and Howard, who was eight.

Holmes moved the children from city to city through the fall and winter, and the children wrote letters as they went, to their mother and their grandparents, ordinary letters of the kind children write when they are far from home and want to come back. Holmes collected the letters and never mailed them. When he was arrested, the letters were among his effects, and they became the map. Detective Frank Geyer of the Philadelphia police took the case that no one else believed would lead anywhere, and he followed the cities the letters named, one after another, across the Midwest and into Canada. In Toronto he found Alice and Nellie. In Irvington, Indiana, near Indianapolis, he found Howard.

I am going to keep the manner of the children's deaths off this page, as the book has kept the worst particulars off the page throughout, and for the same reason. The popular accounts dwell on how the Pitezel children died. This book will not, because there is nothing a reader needs from those particulars that the plain fact does not already give them. Holmes killed all three children. He killed them as part of the same scheme that killed their father, to erase the people who could connect him to it. What belongs on the page is not the method. It is the shape of the thing. A detective crossed a continent to find three children, guided by the letters the children had written and been forbidden to send, and the letters led him to them because the man who took them could not bring himself to throw away the evidence of what he was doing. The kept letter is a trophy, in the sense Chapter 4 gave the word, and like the trophies of Chapter 12 it became the record that convicted the man who kept it.

Holmes was tried in Philadelphia for a single murder, that of Benjamin Pitezel, and convicted of it, and hanged on the seventh of May, 1896. The castle killings in Chicago were investigated only after his arrest, in the sensational atmosphere that followed it, and he was never convicted of any of them. The one murder the law proved against him was the insurance killing, the financial crime, the case built by the ancestors of financial forensics and closed by a detective with a bundle of letters.

How Many, Honestly

The number attached to Holmes is where the legend does its heaviest work, so it is worth stating in the three tiers this book has used from the prologue forward.

Proven, the number is one. Benjamin Pitezel is the murder the law established, the one Holmes was tried and convicted and hanged for. Probable, on the archival evidence, the number is around nine, and every one of the probable victims is a person Holmes knew, which is consistent with everything the record shows about how he actually operated. Confessed, the number reached twenty-seven at one point, in a confession Holmes sold to a newspaper, and here the legend and the liar meet, because several of the people Holmes confessed to murdering turned up alive, and others appear never to have existed at all. Holmes invented victims. A confession from a man who invents victims is not a count. It is a performance. And legend, the number climbs to as many as two hundred, a figure with no evidentiary basis whatsoever, which Selzer traces largely to a 1940 pulp book, Herbert Asbury's Gem of the Prairie, and to the newspaper sensationalism of the eighteen-nineties that Asbury drew on.

One proven. About nine probable. Twenty-seven confessed by a proven liar. Two hundred in the legend. The distance from one to two hundred is the distance this chapter is measuring, and the discipline that measures it, proven over probable over confessed over legend, is the same discipline that separates every real number in this book from every inflated one.

Belle Gunness and the Farm Outside La Porte

If Holmes is the venue that turned out to be legend, Belle Gunness is the venue that turned out to be real, and setting the two side by side is the point of putting them in one chapter.

Belle Gunness was born Brynhild Paulsdatter Storseth in Selbu, Norway, in 1859, the youngest of eight children, and emigrated to the United States in 1881. By the early nineteen-hundreds she was a widow running a farm outside La Porte, Indiana, and she was active, across Illinois and Indiana, from roughly 1884 until 1908. Her motive was the same as Holmes's, money, in her case the cash and the insurance of the men she courted. She was, by the physical descriptions that survive, a large and powerful woman, somewhere around five foot eight and upward of two hundred pounds, and that detail, which seems like color, turns out to be the hinge the whole case swings on.

The venue, in her case, was not a legend. Her farm was a genuinely operational site for killing and disposal. Where Holmes's murder architecture is mostly newspaper invention, the graves on the Gunness property were real, and the bodies were buried in the hog lot and the garden and the grounds, and they were found there. One venue in this chapter is a story. The other is a farm with the dead in the soil. The contrast is the chapter's spine, because it shows that the venue is a real category of forensic fact and also a favorite subject of legend, and that the discipline is what tells the investigator which one is in front of them.

The lure was a standing procedure, and it is the same mechanism this book described in Chapter 12, running half a century earlier. Gunness placed matrimonial advertisements in the Norwegian-language newspapers of the Midwest, inviting a solid, well-off man to come and join his fortune to hers, and requiring, in the way these things were arranged, that he arrive in person and bring his money with him. This is exactly the Gonzalez help-wanted advertisement of Chapter 12, the disarming approach abstracted out of any single encounter and turned into a continuous, advertised process. It is Chapter 4's victim-selection pillar in its most industrialized historical form. The advertisement does the selecting. It brings a steady supply of the right kind of victim, a man with cash and few local ties, to the door of the venue, and the venue does the rest. The ad brings them in and the farm closes around them.

One documented case gives the procedure a face. Andrew Helgelien was a bachelor farmer from Aberdeen, South Dakota. He corresponded with Gunness, and the letters warmed, and one of them, in her hand, closed with an invitation to come prepared to stay forever. He emptied his bank accounts, traveled to La Porte in early 1908, and was never seen alive again. It was Helgelien's disappearance, and specifically the persistence of his brother, that would bring the whole operation into the light.

The Fire, and What the Ground Held

On the twenty-eighth of April, 1908, the Gunness farmhouse burned. In the ruins, searchers found the bodies of an adult woman and three children. The children were Gunness's own, Myrtle and Lucy and Philip. The adult woman's body was missing its head, and it was, at first, assumed to be Belle Gunness.

Andrew Helgelien's brother, Asle Helgelien, had been writing and pressing about his missing brother for some time, unsatisfied with the answers he was getting from La Porte. His inquiries, arriving at the same moment as the fire, turned suspicion toward the farm itself, and the grounds were searched. The search unearthed the partial remains of at least eleven more people. The total recovered from the property ran well over a dozen, and Andrew Helgelien was among the dead. The farm had been what the letters and the advertisements implied it was all along.

Ray Lamphere, a former handyman on the farm who had a complicated history with Gunness, was tried in connection with the fire. He was convicted of arson, not murder, and he implicated Gunness in the deaths without being convicted of them himself. The forensic work here is once again the older, wider kind: a missing-person inquiry pressed by a stubborn brother, a fire, and a search of the ground with shovels. No laboratory. A brother who would not stop asking, and the dead in the garden.

The Body That Was Too Small

Here the case turns, on the physical detail that seemed like mere description a moment ago. The headless adult woman found in the burned farmhouse was too small to be Belle Gunness. Gunness was a large woman, close to five foot eight and around two hundred pounds. The body in the ruins was several inches shorter and far lighter, and the discrepancy was noticed at the time and never went away. It fed a belief, which has lasted more than a century, that Gunness set the fire herself, left a substitute body in her place, and escaped.

The question has never been closed. A great deal has been written attempting to settle it, and in 2007 and 2008 a team exhumed the body believed to be Gunness and attempted to identify it through DNA. The attempt was inconclusive. We do not know, to the standard this book requires, whether the woman in the grave is Belle Gunness or another woman who died in her place. We do not know whether Gunness died in 1908 or lived on for years under another name. Her death toll and her ultimate fate are both, to this day, open questions.

This is the undercount problem and the myth-versus-record problem meeting in a single figure. The count is unknowable at the top for the oldest reasons in the book, the same reasons it recurs with Samuel Little in Chapter 9: victims who were transient and marginalized, men who had told the people back home they were leaving to start a new life and so were not quickly missed, primitive record-keeping, and a site organized for concealment. And the fate is unknowable because the one piece of physical evidence that should have answered it, the body, does not match the woman it was supposed to be. Gunness is a case where the record runs out before the questions do, and the honest thing, which is also the disciplined thing, is to say so and stop, rather than to fill the silence with a story.

In the three tiers, then. Recovered from the farm, well over a dozen, the four who died in the fire plus at least eleven more sets of remains taken from the grounds, Andrew Helgelien among them. Suspected, roughly twenty-five to forty, across the decades and the two states. And in the press and the legend, over forty, with some contemporary accounts reaching higher still. The recovered figure is the one that rests on remains in the ground. The rest is estimate and story, and it is marked as such.

What the Venue Teaches

Two cases, a continent and a couple of decades apart, one venue that was a legend and one that was a farm. Set them together and they teach four things, and every one of them reaches forward into the modern cases this book has already covered.

The controlled venue is an anchor point, and it is old. A space the offender owns and governs removes the practical limits that constrain a crime committed in the open. It gives privacy, time, control, and a place to put the dead. That is why the venue recurs across eras and reappears in Chapter 12 as the Bittaker van, the Lake bunker, and the Gonzalez ranch. Holmes and Gunness are the historical head of that lineage. The building and the farm are the ancestors of the van and the bunker, and the logic is identical across the century that separates them. Control the space and the limits fall away.

The lure becomes a standing procedure. Gunness's matrimonial advertisements are the Gonzalez help-wanted advertisements of Chapter 12, running fifty years earlier, the same disarming approach turned into an advertised, continuous process that delivers the right victims to the door. The venue and the lure are partners. The advertisement brings them in, and the venue closes around them, and the two mechanisms together are more efficient and more sustainable than either would be alone. This is a machine, in a sense the murder castle never was, and Gunness actually built it.

The undercount problem is oldest here. Both of these counts are unknowable at the top end, and for the reasons the problem always recurs, the ones Chapter 9 laid out with Samuel Little. The victims were transient, marginalized, or deliberately severed from the people who would miss them. The record-keeping of the era was primitive. And the sites were organized for concealment. When those conditions hold, the count floats, and the honest practitioner reports the floor and marks everything above it as estimate.

And the lesson that belongs to this chapter more than any other in the book: the venue legend outruns the evidence. Holmes is the proof. The murder castle, the machine built to kill strangers by the score, is largely invention, and the real Holmes was a financial predator who controlled a building and killed the people his schemes required him to kill. A chapter that could have been the most lurid in the book turns out instead to be its clearest demonstration of method, because the discipline the book preaches, proven over probable over confessed over legend, is exactly the tool that separates the real Holmes from the tall tale. The legend is more exciting. The record is more interesting, and it is also true.

Which returns to where the chapter began. Neither of these killers was caught by a crime laboratory, because there was not one yet. Holmes was caught by the ancestors of financial and documentary forensics, by an insurer's suspicion and a money trail and a bundle of kept letters and a detective who followed them across a continent. Gunness's farm gave up its dead to a stubborn brother's missing-person inquiry and a search of the ground. Forensics is older and wider than the laboratory, older than the word most people attach to it, and this chapter is where the book says so plainly. The lab, when it came in 1923, organized and sharpened and standardized a family of disciplines that were already generations old and had already, in the eighteen-nineties and the nineteen-hundreds, caught two of the most notorious killers in American history. The science had been at work long before it had a building to work in.

ON THE RECORD

Established

- **Holmes was a financial criminal who murdered for money, and was convicted of exactly one murder.** Benjamin Pitezel, an insurance-fraud killing, was the crime the law proved. Holmes was hanged for it on May 7, 1896. The Chicago castle crimes were never the basis of his conviction.

- **The murder castle is largely a newspaper invention.** Per Adam Selzer's archival history, the building was not a working hotel, the third floor was never finished or opened, and the hidden spaces appear to have concealed furniture bought on credit rather than victims. There is no evidence of gas chambers or a dissection lab.
- **Holmes was caught by the ancestors of financial and documentary forensics, decades before the crime lab.** An insurer's suspicion, a money trail, penetrated aliases, a jailhouse tip, and a set of kept letters that let Detective Frank Geyer trace the Pitezel children. The first US crime lab did not exist until 1923.
- **Gunness's venue was real and her lure was a standing procedure.** The farm outside La Porte held the dead in its grounds, and Gunness recruited victims through matrimonial advertisements, the same advertised-lure mechanism seen in Chapter 12, running half a century earlier.

Myth

- **That Holmes killed as many as two hundred strangers in a purpose-built murder hotel.** The proven count is one; the defensible estimate is about nine, all people he knew. The two-hundred figure traces to 1890s sensationalism and a 1940 pulp book, not to evidence, and the popular picture crystallized by The Devil in the White City rests on those inflated contemporary sources.
- **That Holmes's confessions are a victim count.** He confessed to twenty-seven at one point, but several supposed victims turned up alive and others appear to have been invented. A confession from a man who invents victims is a performance, not a tally.

Still unsettled

- **Whether Belle Gunness died in the 1908 fire.** The headless body in the ruins was too small to be her, which fed a lasting belief that she escaped. A 2007 to 2008 DNA exhumation was inconclusive. Her fate remains open.
- **The true victim counts for both offenders.** Holmes: one proven, about nine probable. Gunness: well over a dozen recovered,

roughly twenty-five to forty suspected. The tops of both ranges are unknowable for the oldest reasons in the book, and are marked as estimate.

Chapter 14: Synthesis: How We Know

This book began in a garage.

A false wall, plywood and clutter arranged to read as the back of the room, built to push away rather than swing open. Behind it, nearly a thousand photographs and hundreds of hours of video, organized in the way a person organizes something he means to keep and to return to. And elsewhere in the same house, not hidden behind anything, the gun from the last murder, left out in the open. The thing worth concealing was the record. The murder weapon was not.

I opened on that room because it holds, in a single image, the argument this whole book has been making. A man built a wall to hide the one thing he could not make himself throw away, and left the weapon lying in plain sight, and in that inversion he told the people searching his house exactly what mattered to him and exactly what did not. He behaved like a person who kept souvenirs, because that is what he was. And that behavior, the keeping, the concealment, the habit he could not break across twenty-five years, is the kind of thing that ends a case.

The question I posed in that room was the one the entire book has been answering. Not why he did it. That is a different book, written by people with a different training, and I have stayed out of that lane on purpose from the first page to this one. The question I spent a career on is the other one. How do we know? How does a series of murders, separated by years and neighborhoods and jurisdictions, separated sometimes by decades and by investigative teams who never spoke because they had no reason to think there was anything to speak about, get identified as the work of one person? A woman killed in 1985 and a woman killed in 2002 are two unrelated homicides in a city that has thousands of them, until somebody establishes that they are not.

Now, with the whole book behind us, I can answer the question plainly, in a way the prologue could only pose. This chapter is where the pieces go back together.

What the Pillars Are For

The title of this book is By the Same Hand, and it is time to say directly what it means, because everything in these pages has been building toward it. The book has been about a single question the whole time. The question is common authorship. Were these crimes committed by the same hand? Every chapter, whatever its ostensible subject, has been an examination of how that one question gets answered.

The four pillars are not four separate lessons. They are four inputs to that one decision. This is the thing I most want a reader to carry away, because it is the thing the standard presentation gets wrong by treating the pillars as a checklist or a personality sketch. They are neither. The comfort zone, the signature, the trophies, and the victim selection are four independent readings of the same crime, and the reason to take all four is that they can be checked against one another. Linkage is the through-line of this entire book. It ran under the prologue, under every case chapter, under the historical cases and the team cases and the ones the discipline could not close. The pillars exist to serve it. They are how a practitioner moves from two files on two desks to one offender with one set of habits, and the movement from the first state to the second is the whole of the work.

The Four Readings, Taken Together

Consider what each pillar actually contributes to the linkage decision, not as a definition this time but as a function, because the functions are what let them corroborate and contradict one another.

The comfort zone narrows the geography and points at the anchor. It tells the practitioner where the offender was operating from, what territory he moved through without friction, and, when it is a constructed venue rather than a familiar area, what physical place the crimes were organized around. The signature establishes authorship. It is the element that persists when the method changes, the thing the offender does because he needs to rather than because the crime requires it, and it is therefore the reading that most directly answers the same-hand question. The trophies and the documentation confirm, and increasingly they convict, because a kept record is both the proof that the offender could not let go and, once recovered, the evidence that closes the case. And the victim selection reveals access. It tells the practitioner who the offender could reach without raising the alarm that ends the encounter, and that in turn points back at the offender's world, his work, his social range, his zone.

Four readings of one crime. The power is not in any single one. It is in what happens when they are laid over each other, because they can agree, and they can disagree, and both of those tell the practitioner something.

The Grim Sleeper is the clean read, the case where the pillars all point one way once the evidence holds. The killings ran across an apparent gap of more than a decade, and the method drifted in those years, enough that the early cluster and the later cluster read on the surface as separate offenders. But the comfort zone held, the same few square miles of South Los Angeles. The victim selection held, the same access to the same vulnerable population. The documentation, when it was finally found behind that garage wall, held in the most literal way imaginable, an archive of the victims themselves. And the signature and the physical evidence held, because when the DNA from an early victim was matched to the later cluster, the apparent gap collapsed and the pillars aligned. Every reading pointed at one hand. That is what the clean case looks like, and it is worth remembering that the clean case still took twenty-five years to close, because the readings only align once someone has done the work of gathering them.

Clark and Bundy is the hard read, the case where the pillars resist a clean answer and the discipline is to hold the model loosely. The dominant-and-compliant structure that organized every other team in this book did not map cleanly onto them. The physical evidence cut against the obvious story, the murder weapon registered to the partner the narrative wanted to cast as passive, the trophies in her keeping rather than his. The pillars, read honestly, did not output a verdict. They produced a tension that had to be held rather than resolved, and the honest practitioner holds it. This is the case I would give anyone who wants to understand what the pillars are and are not. They are inputs to a judgment. They are not a formula that returns an answer when you feed it a crime. When they disagree, the disagreement is data, and the practitioner who forces a clean reading onto a case that will not support one has stopped doing forensics and started telling a story.

And the venue and the lure read correctly across a century, which is the last thing the reassembled pillars demonstrate. The controlled venue that opens the modern team cases, the Bittaker van, the Lake bunker, the Gonzalez ranch, is the same category of anchor as the Gunness farm and, in its legend, the Holmes castle, and the pillar reads the same in 1908 and in 1985. The advertised lure that Gunness ran in the Norwegian-language papers is the same mechanism the Gonzalez sisters ran in the help-wanted columns half a century later, and the same access logic Chapter 4 defined in the present tense. The pillars are not artifacts of a particular decade or a particular technology. They describe how this kind of offender behaves, and the behavior has been consistent for as long as there has been a record to read it in. That consistency is what makes linkage possible at all. If offenders did not repeat themselves, there would be nothing to link.

What Actually Feeds the Decision

Chapter 13 made the argument that forensics is a wide federation of disciplines and that the crime-lab bench most people picture is one sliver of it. That argument pays off here, because the linkage decision is fed by the whole federation, and only a fraction of it looks like what television has taught people to expect.

Linkage analysis itself is the discipline that sits at the center, the structured comparison of crimes across the exact factors this book has spent its length describing. Around it sits the rest of the family. Documentation and forensic photography, the recording of a scene completely enough that a question no one thought to ask at the time can be answered years later from the record, which is the discipline that preserved a fingernail's worth of tissue in 1989 and a thousand photographs in 2010. DNA analysis and the databases that let a profile from one scene be run against profiles from many others, which is the tool that collapsed the Grim Sleeper's apparent gap. Financial and documentary forensics, the reading of money trails and papers and aliases, which is the ancestral discipline that caught Holmes a generation before there was a laboratory. Pattern and impression evidence, ballistics and toolmarks and the rest, which tied the Grim Sleeper's clusters together at the level of the weapon. Toxicology, odontology, forensic anthropology, each feeding the decision from its own angle.

My own lane was documentation, forensic photography, one of the disciplines that does not look like the bench and is forensic science all the same. I have spent this book arguing that the family is wider than the popular picture, and I will note once more, and then let it go, that I spent a career inside one of its rooms, and that the room was not the lab, and that the work done there was as much a part of catching these offenders as anything that happened under a microscope. The federation is real, and the linkage decision draws on all of it.

The Honest Count

One discipline has run through this book as a habit, and I want to close by raising it from habit to principle, because it is the ethic that separates method from legend. Every count in these pages has been stated in tiers. Proven. Probable or suspected. Confessed. Legend. Each labeled as what it is, and never blurred into a single dramatic number.

The reason is on the page in every chapter that used it. Holmes, one murder proven against two hundred in the legend, and the distance between those two numbers is the distance between forensic method and newspaper invention. Gunness, well over a dozen recovered from the ground and an unknowable number above that, a floor that rests on remains and a ceiling that rests on estimate. Samuel Little, the undercount problem in its fullest form, a man who was in the end a more reliable witness to the existence of his own victims than the systems that were supposed to be counting them. In each case the discipline is the same. The practitioner reports the floor, the number that rests on evidence, and marks everything above it as estimate, and refuses to let the estimate harden into a fact merely because it is more dramatic.

This is not pedantry, and it is not modesty for its own sake. It is part of respecting the victims, and it is part of getting at the truth, and in this work those two things are the same thing. An inflated count buries the real victims under invented ones and tells the families of the real victims that the truth of what happened to their people is less important than the size of the legend. A false ceiling is a disservice to everyone under it. The honest count, the floor stated plainly and the estimate marked as estimate, is what a true accounting looks like, and a true accounting is the least the dead are owed. The disciplined practitioner counts honestly precisely because the victims deserve the truth rather than the drama.

Why the Method Exists

Which brings the book to the thing it has been walking toward from the garage on the first page. Why does any of it exist? Not the pillars for their own sake, not the linkage as a puzzle to be admired, not the offender as a figure of fascination. The method exists for the people on the other side of the crime.

There was a billboard in South Los Angeles with faces in a row across the top, each with a name and a year. Debra Jackson, 1985. Henrietta Wright, 1986. Thomas Steele, 1987. Barbara Ware, 1987. Bernita Sparks, 1987. Mary Lowe, 1987. Lachrica Jefferson, 1988. Alicia Alexander, 1988. Princess Berthomieux, 2002. Valerie McCorvey, 2003. Janecia Peters, 2007. And a silhouette, for the one who survived and whose name is hers to give or withhold rather than mine. Those names are the reason. Not the man behind the wall. The people whose faces were behind it.

I sat in a room with some of their families before the first trial, brought there, I came to understand, because the forensic staff were the people who had gathered the evidence and made sure it was gathered properly, and were trusted in a community with reason to trust the police less than they should have been able to. What I carried out of that room is the thing I want to leave a reader with. Forensic professionals do not want a killer caught. They want the killer caught. Not merely someone who can be convicted of being the killer, but the actual person who did it, established to a standard that will hold, so that the answer delivered to the people in that room is the true one. Everything in this book, the pillars, the linkage, the wide federation, the honest count, exists in service of that. The discipline is not the point. The true answer, delivered to the people who are owed it, is the point. The discipline is only how you earn the right to stand in that room and say the name of the person who did this, and be right.

So the book ends where it began, in a garage, in front of a wall a man built to hide the record of what he had done. He built it because he could not throw the record away, and because he could not throw it away, it was found, and because it was found, the people whose faces were behind it were not, in the end, entirely lost. That is what the same hand leaves behind. That is why the question at the front of this book, how do we know, is worth a career and worth a book. We know because the offender, whatever else he is, is a creature of habit who keeps what he cannot bear to discard, and because there are people whose work it is to read what he leaves. The reading is the method. The method is for the victims. And the wall, in the end, comes down.

How the reading is changing, and how the people who do it hope to get faster at it, so that the next wall comes down in years instead of decades, is the last thing left to say. That is where this turns next.

ON THE RECORD

Established

- **The four pillars are four inputs to one decision, not four separate lessons.** Comfort zone, signature, trophies, and victim selection are independent readings of the same crime, and their value lies in being checked against one another. The decision they feed is common authorship, which is the through-line of the entire book.
- **The pillars corroborate and contradict, and both are informative.** The Grim Sleeper is the clean read where every pillar aligned once the DNA held. Clark and Bundy is the hard read where the pillars resisted a clean answer and the discipline was to hold the model loosely. The pillars are inputs to a judgment, not a formula that returns a verdict.
- **The linkage decision is fed by the whole forensic federation, most of which is not the crime-lab bench.** Linkage analysis, documentation and forensic photography, DNA and its databases, financial and documentary forensics, and pattern evidence all feed it. The bench is one part of a wide family.
- **The honest count is an ethic, not a device.** The practitioner reports the floor that rests on evidence and marks everything above it as estimate, because the victims are owed a true accounting rather

than a dramatic one. Proven over probable over confessed over legend.

Myth

- **That the pillars are a checklist or a personality profile.** They are neither. They are four evidentiary readings whose agreement or disagreement informs a judgment about common authorship. Treated as a formula, they produce stories rather than conclusions.
- **That forensics solves cases on its own.** It narrows and confirms; it rarely solves alone. Gunness may have walked. Lake and Ng broke on a shoplifting arrest. The Grim Sleeper ran for a quarter of a century before the linkage held. Plenty still gets away.

Still unsettled

- **How much still goes uncounted.** The undercount problem that runs from Samuel Little through the historical cases has no known floor beneath the floor. The method reveals what it can reach, and is honest about what it cannot.
- **Why offenders keep what convicts them.** That the keeping happens is established and is the most useful single fact in this book. Why a person builds a wall to hide the evidence he cannot make himself destroy is a question of a kind this book has deliberately left to others.

Epilogue: So What's Next

I spent a good part of my career watching one forensic technology be born, and I want to start there, because it is the closest thing I have to a qualification for the rest of this chapter.

When I came into forensic and operational photography, the work was done on film. You exposed it, you developed it, you printed it, and the chain of custody ran through physical negatives that a person could hold up to the light. I was there when digital arrived, and I mean genuinely there at the front of it. In the Air Force, working Combat Camera, I was deployed to the Bosnian war effort using some of the first digital cameras available, in the field, on real operations, at a time when a digital image was not yet accepted in a courtroom at all and nobody had settled what it would take for one to be. That was the leading edge, and standing on it taught me something I carried for the rest of my career: a new imaging technology shows up useful long before anyone has worked out how to make it trustworthy, and the gap between those two things is where all the hard work lives.

Later, at the Los Angeles Police Department, I ran the analog-to-digital conversion for the photographic operation, and I wrote manuals for it, and I sat on the national standards bodies that were trying to figure out, in real time, how a digital image could be trusted in a courtroom the way a negative had been. I chaired the forensic photography committee of two of those bodies. The question we were answering was not whether digital was better. It obviously was. The question was how to make it trustworthy, because a digital image can be altered in ways a negative cannot, and a discipline that could not answer the how-do-we-trust-it question was going to get its evidence thrown out and deserve it.

So I have watched a forensic technology go through the whole cycle. The promise, when it was new and exciting and oversold. The backlash, when people realized it could be manipulated and trust collapsed. And finally the standards, the slow unglamorous work of writing the rules that let the technology be believed again, on the right terms, with its limits stated honestly and accepted in Court. Every technology in this chapter is somewhere on that same cycle, and I read all of them through the one I lived. That is the lens. Now the forecast, in two parts, what is arriving and what is leaving, with the usual warning that a practitioner making predictions is a practitioner setting himself up to be quoted back to later. I will take that risk, and I will mark the speculation as speculation where it belongs.

What Is Arriving

The largest change coming to forensic evidence over the next several years is that DNA analysis is moving beyond the single trick it has done since the nineteen-eighties. The DNA profiling this book has referred to throughout, the kind that matched the Grim Sleeper across a decade and named Samuel Little's victims, works by comparing a small number of repeating markers, and it answers essentially one question: does this sample match this person. That question is enormously powerful, and it is not going away. But a family of newer techniques is arriving that asks different questions, and the shorthand for the whole family is the omics, from genomics and the disciplines that have grown up beside it.

Next-generation sequencing is the near-term workhorse. Instead of measuring the length of DNA fragments, it reads the actual sequence, letter by letter, which lets an examiner pull usable information from samples that are degraded or mixed together in ways that defeat the older method. A mixture of two or three people's DNA, which can be a nightmare to interpret with the current tools, becomes more tractable. This one is not speculative. Commercial platforms are already validated and in use.

DNA phenotyping is further out and more contested. It attempts to predict what a person looks like from crime-scene DNA, eye color, hair color, some ancestry, the rough outlines of facial structure, for cases where there is a sample but no database match to compare it against. Used carefully, it can narrow a field. Used carelessly, it can point an investigation at everyone who shares a set of common traits, which is a great many innocent people, and that risk is real enough that the technique deserves the caution it gets.

Forensic epigenetics is the one I find most interesting, because it reads not the DNA sequence itself but the chemical marks layered on top of it, and those marks change with age and circumstance. That means a sample can, increasingly, be made to estimate how old the person who left it was, and even roughly how old the sample itself is, whether a stain was left days ago or years ago. A recent marker set has been reported to estimate age across a wide range with growing accuracy. For a cold case, the ability to say that a decades-old sample came from a person who was in a particular age range at the time is a genuinely new kind of lead.

The microbiome is arriving alongside it. Every person carries a distinctive community of microorganisms, and so does every place, and the soil on a shoe carries a signature specific enough to distinguish one location from another. The forensic uses are early but real, linking a person to a place, estimating how long a body has been where it was found, potentially even distinguishing individuals. Proteomics and the analysis of RNA round out the family, offering ways to identify body fluids reliably and to read information from samples like hair where the DNA itself has broken down but proteins survive.

And then there is artificial intelligence, which I want to handle carefully, because it is the item on this list most surrounded by noise and the one I have been asked about most and seen documented least. The promise, specific to this book, is linkage. An artificial intelligence trained on the behavioral and situational details of many crimes could, in principle, spot the connections between cases that a human analyst might miss, and spot them earlier, which is the whole game, because the linkage gap is what let the offenders in this book run for as long as they did. The honest picture of where this actually stands is narrower than the marketing suggests. The most credible deployment I am aware of is not in the United States but in the United Kingdom, where the National Crime Agency's specialist analysis unit has an artificial-intelligence-assisted linkage tool that has been put into real operational use and then studied, in the open, by researchers. The studies found something that fits everything this book has argued. The analysts wanted the tool to show its work, to present the evidence alongside its suggestion rather than handing down a conclusion from inside a black box, because a suggestion they could not examine was a suggestion they could not trust or defend. That, and not the accuracy number, is the thing to watch. An artificial intelligence that links crimes and cannot show why it linked them is the pattern-matching examiner's old overclaim in a new and faster costume, and it will have to meet the same standard everything else in this chapter meets. The predictions of very high accuracy that appear in the literature come, so far, from controlled conditions on selected data, which is the laboratory's way of saying not yet proven in the field. My read, and I mark it as a read, is that this tool is real and coming and will help, and that the version of it worth having is the version that assists a human judgment instead of replacing it, and shows its reasoning every time.

What Is Leaving

The more surprising forecast, and the more overdue one, is on the other side of the ledger. Several forensic disciplines that have sent people to prison for decades are being dismantled, slowly and against heavy institutional resistance, because they were never scientifically valid in the first place. Understanding why requires naming the document that has done more than any other to force the reckoning.

In September of 2016, the President's Council of Advisors on Science and Technology, a federal advisory body of senior scientists that reports to the President, published a report titled Forensic Science in Criminal Courts: Ensuring Scientific Validity of Feature-Comparison Methods. It is known in the field simply as the PCAST report, after the council's initials, and it did something that had not been done with authority before. It asked, of each of the major pattern-comparison disciplines, a single hard question: is there actual scientific evidence, in the form of properly designed studies measuring how often examiners get it wrong, that this method works? It called the property it was testing for foundational validity, and foundational validity is just the scientific way of asking whether a discipline can do what its practitioners claim it can do, at a measured and acknowledged error rate, rather than on the strength of an examiner's confidence.

The findings were not kind. Of the disciplines it examined, the council found that only DNA analysis of single-source and simple two-person samples, and latent fingerprint analysis, met the standard for foundational validity. The others, bite-mark analysis, hair microscopy, footwear comparison, and firearms and toolmark identification, were found to lack sufficient scientific support for the certainty with which they had been presented in court for decades. The report was non-binding, and it was fiercely resisted by parts of the law enforcement and forensic establishment, including formal rebuttals from the Department of Justice and the FBI. But it could not be unpublished, and it handed defense attorneys and courts a scientifically grounded basis for challenging evidence that had been treated as close to infallible. That is why it matters. It changed what could be said with a straight face in a courtroom.

Bite-mark analysis is the clearest casualty and deserves to be. The idea that a person can be identified by matching a bite on a victim to the dentition of a suspect has no scientific foundation, error rates that are catastrophic when they have been measured at all, and a documented trail of wrongful convictions behind it, some of which put innocent people on death row before DNA cleared them. Even former leaders of the professional body that once certified bite-mark examiners have turned against the discipline. No American court has yet ruled it categorically inadmissible, which is its own kind of scandal, but it is dying by challenge, case by case, and it should be dead.

Microscopic hair comparison is nearly as bad. In 2015 the FBI acknowledged that its own examiners had given scientifically flawed testimony in the overwhelming majority of cases its review examined, overstating what a microscopic comparison of hairs could establish. Without a DNA analysis to accompany it, the microscopic matching of hair is no longer something a careful practitioner will stand behind. Firearms and toolmark identification and footwear comparison sit in a more contested middle ground, with firearms examination having somewhat more empirical support than the others, but all of them now testify, or should, in far more careful and qualified language than the certainty they once claimed.

And then there is the fingerprint, which surprises people, so it is worth being precise. Fingerprint analysis was one of the two disciplines the PCAST report found foundationally valid, so it is not going anywhere. What is going away, or should be, is the overclaim. For roughly a century, fingerprint examiners testified to matches with absolute certainty, as identifications to the exclusion of every other person on earth, with an implied error rate of zero. That claim was never supported by science. When the error rate was finally measured in controlled studies, it was small but it was emphatically not zero, with one well-known laboratory study finding false-positive rates on the order of one in a few hundred, and another suggesting they could run higher still under some conditions. A false-positive rate of a few tenths of a percent is perfectly good evidence. It is simply not the certainty a jury was told it was hearing for a hundred years. The fingerprint is not leaving. The lie that it is infallible is, and its departure is overdue.

Closing the Gap

Set the two sides of the ledger next to each other and a direction emerges. The disciplines that are arriving share a property, and it is the property the disciplines that are leaving lacked. The new tools are built to state their error rates, to acknowledge their limits, to show their work. That is not a coincidence. It is the whole lesson of the last twenty years of forensic science, learned the hard way, over the bodies of the people who were wrongly convicted by methods that claimed a certainty they never had.

What all of it is for, in the end, is closing the gap this book has been circling from the first page. The Grim Sleeper ran for a quarter of a century, across a detection gap that was not a gap in his activity but a gap in the linking of his crimes. Samuel Little ran for something like half a century, uncounted, because the system that should have connected his victims never did. The offenders in this book were not caught late because the science failed when it was finally applied. They were caught late because the linkage came late, because too much time passed between the crimes and the moment someone established that the crimes belonged together. Every technology arriving in the next several years, the sequencing and the phenotyping and the epigenetic clocks and, if it grows up honestly, the artificial intelligence, points at the same target: closing that gap. Making the linkage sooner. Catching the series at the fifth victim instead of the fiftieth.

If these tools deliver even part of what they promise, there will be fewer billboards that go up too late, with faces on them that no one can name anymore because thirty years have passed. There will be fewer families waiting a quarter of a century for an answer. There will be fewer women in a compartment behind a wall whose names are lost to time. That is the promise, and it is worth being hopeful about, with the discipline that the hope has to survive contact with the evidence, the same as everything else in this book.

I will end where I began, with the cycle I watched. Digital photography arrived in my field oversold and half-trusted, and it took years of unglamorous work, standards and manuals and validation and argument, to make it into the reliable forensic tool it is now. Every technology in this chapter will go through the same passage. Each will arrive oversold. Each will disappoint someone. Each will be challenged, and the ones that survive the challenge will survive it by doing what the discredited disciplines never did, by stating honestly what they can and cannot do and proving it with data. I have seen this happen once, from the inside, for one technology. I expect to see the beginning of it happen several more times, and I will not be around for the end of most of them, which is fine. That is how the field works. It is slow, and it is adversarial, and it is self-correcting on a timescale measured in careers rather than cases, and it grinds toward getting the truth right because the cost of getting it wrong is a person's life.

The tools will keep changing. What will not change is the question they all serve, the one from the garage on the first page of this book. How do we know two crimes were committed by the same hand. Whatever answers that question faster, and answers it honestly, with its error rate stated and its reasoning shown, is the future of this work. Everything else is a costume. The method outlasts the technology, because the method is not the machine. It is the discipline of asking what the evidence can actually support, and refusing to claim one inch more than that. That discipline caught a financial predator in 1894 with a bundle of letters, and it caught a man behind a false wall in 2010 with a database and a photograph, and it will catch the next one with tools neither of us can picture yet. The tools are new every generation. The question is always the same. And the answer, when we get it right, still comes down to the same quiet, careful, unglamorous work it always has.

About the Author

I spent thirty-four years making photographs that other people needed to trust.

I started in the United States Air Force in 1982 and stayed until 1996. Along the way I ran quality control and trained photographers, I worked the continuous-image processing for the SR-71, TR-1, and U-2 reconnaissance programs, and I served as a team leader in Combat Camera, deployed to the Bosnian war effort out of Aviano Air Base in Italy. It was in that deployment that I first put my hands on the earliest digital cameras, in the field, on real operations, at a time when nobody had yet decided what a digital image was worth as a record. That turned out to be the beginning of a thread I would follow for the rest of my working life, the question of how a new way of capturing an image earns the right to be believed.

In 1998 I joined the Los Angeles Police Department's Scientific Investigation Division, where I spent the next two decades. I became a supervisor, directing a staff of twelve on a unit that ran around the clock, and I was responsible for the photography and videography of the department's high-profile criminal and civil cases. I oversaw the department's conversion from film to digital, wrote the operations manuals that governed it, and represented the LAPD on the national bodies that were writing the standards for forensic imaging as the field remade itself. I served on the Scientific Working Group on Imaging Technologies and later the Scientific Working Group on Digital Evidence, both FBI working groups, and I chaired the forensic photography committee. I was qualified as an expert witness in forensic photography. That standards work and that testimony are not glamorous, and they are the reason the images I am about to describe held up in court.

I was the initial and primary photographer on the Robert Blake case. I led a team of five photographers documenting the Grim Sleeper case, which is the investigation this book is built around and one of the most prolific serial murder cases in American history. And I provided the photographic analysis and forensic work in the Lisker case, part of the effort that freed Bruce Lisker after twenty-three years in prison for a murder he did not commit. I put those three together deliberately, because they describe the range of what this work is for. Sometimes the evidence convicts a guilty man. Sometimes, done honestly, it frees an innocent one. The discipline is the same in both directions, and it has to be, because the moment it bends toward the outcome someone wants, it stops being evidence and becomes something else.

I am not a profiler and I am not a forensic psychologist. I have stayed out of the question of why these offenders did what they did, deliberately and completely, because it is not my field and there are people better equipped to answer it. The question I spent a career on is the other one, the one this book is about. How do we know? How does a photograph, a fingerprint, a piece of evidence documented correctly at a scene, become the thread that ties a series of crimes to a single hand? I learned the answer to that question one case at a time, in garages and at crime scenes and on a witness stand, and this book is my attempt to set it down plainly for anyone who wants to understand how it actually works, rather than how it looks on television.

I retired from the Los Angeles Police Department and became an author, still convinced that the most important work in a criminal case is often the quietest, done by people whose names never appear in the story. This book is, among other things, for them.

www.ingramcontent.com/pod-product-compliance
Lightning Source LLC
LaVergne TN
LVHW100730061126
851857LV00011B/463
9798994037782